Child Development
An illustrated guide

Carolyn Meggitt

www.heinemann.co.uk

✓ Free online support
✓ Useful weblinks
✓ 24 hour online ordering

01865 888058

Heinemann

Inspiring generations

Heinemann Educational Publishers
Halley Court, Jordan Hill, Oxford OX2 8EJ
Part of Harcourt Education

Heinemann is the registered trademark of
Harcourt Education Limited

First published 2000
Second edition published 2006

10 09 08 07
10 9 8 7 6 5

British Library Cataloguing in Publication Data is available
from the British Library on request.

13-digit ISBN: 978 0 435420 48 2

Produced by Wooden Ark Ltd

Original illustrations © Harcourt Education Limited, 2005

Cover design by Wooden Ark Ltd
Printed in China through Phoenix Offset
Cover photo: © Jules Selmes
Picture research by Jane Hance
Photographs: © Harcourt Education Ltd / Jules Selmes

Acknowledgements

Every effort has been made to contact copyright holders of material reproduced in this book. Any
omissions will be rectified in subsequent printings if notice is given to the publishers.

Contents

Contents

Acknowledgements

I would like to thank the following people for their valuable assistance in producing this book: the parents of all the babies and children whose photographs appear in the book; the children for their patience and co-operation; all the staff at Asquith Nursery Trafalgar, Twickenham, for their invaluable help: especially to Georgina Llewellyn, Senior Nursery Manager; Asha Bagha, Nursery Deputy; Julie Cowell, Nursery Room Supervisor; Natalie Hunt, Nursery Nurse, and Anna Tomlinson, pre-School Teacher.

Many thanks to all the children and parents at Maidstone Children's Centre for the photographs in the section on children with special needs; also to all the staff there, including: Mary Board, Nursery manager; Pauline Johnson, Physiotherapist; Janet Davey, Staff Nurse; Sam Gibbs and Mireille Ford, Specialist Nursery Nurses; Pat Heath, Technical Instructor, and Susan Watts, Student Nurse LD.

Also, a big thank you to Jules Selmes for his patience and skill in taking all the photographs in the book, and to David Yems for helping to ensure that the photo shoots went so smoothly.

Thanks to the publishing team at Heinemann Educational for their efficiency and enthusiasm – to Beth Howard, Publisher; Lucy Hyde, Managing Editor; Jane Hance, Picture Researcher, and to Alex Gray and Charlotte Rundall, Copy Editors.

This book is

dedicated to

Jake Oliver Wiseman

Foreword

The first edition of this book has been a great support to practitioners working directly with children. This second edition, updated and expanded, is very timely and welcome.

The book takes a truly holistic approach, which not only includes a detailed look at the first year of life – important in itself – but also contains chapters on the years from eight to twelve and from twelve to sixteen. This is unusual, and very helpful in establishing what is important in influencing the life journeys children take over time.

Throughout the book, there are beautiful photographs illustrating in diverse and inclusive ways the importance of learning through direct experience, movement, exercise and healthy eating. The book is a pleasure to look at and browse through, as well as containing important detail for study of the kind which develops practice. The practical suggestions help readers to make sense of what is written in the guidelines and shown in the charts and photographs.

In the second section of the book, there is greater detail to help the reader understand the importance of developmental assessment. The chapter on special needs is an important one, and everything in the book is underpinned by the accessibly written and presented chapter on some of the most influential theories of child development.

I commend this second edition of the book to readers, and hope you will enjoy finding your way around it and using it as much as I have.

Tina Bruce
Honorary Visiting Professor
Faculty of Humanities and Education (Early Childhood Education)
University of North London

Introduction

The idea for the first edition of this book was conceived in response to the growth of child-care courses worldwide. Many books focused on child development, but no other educational book offered a concise pictorial guide to the general development of children from birth right through to the age of 8 years. In response to the recent development of courses to include child development to the age of 16, this second edition has two new chapters: From Eight to Twelve years and Twelve to Sixteen years. There are also new sections on healthy eating guidelines and on the use of ICT. In addition, the new chapter summarising the main theories of child development will enable students to relate each stage of development to the relevant theory.

Children across the world seem to pass through the same sequences of development, and within the same broad timetables. Although the pattern is generally the same for all children, it is important to remember that each child is unique. Nevertheless, understanding the typical pattern will help you to develop your skills both in promoting children's health and in stimulating their all-round (or holistic) development.

The different areas of development are interrelated. The ideas, language, communication, feelings, relationships and other cultural elements among which each child is brought up influence his or her development profoundly.

Children with special needs often seem to dance the developmental ladder – they move through developmental stages in unusual and very uneven ways. For example, they might sit or walk at the usual age, but not talk at the usual age.

Mary Sheridan's valuable research in the 1950s provides a useful framework for the study of child development. This book extends Sheridan's work by incorporating additional research from many other experts in the field.

Simply reading statements about what a child at a given age is expected to achieve can prove very dull. I believe that presenting this information alongside photographs of real children will bring the subject of child development alive.

Carolyn Meggitt

Using this book

Using this book has many benefits

Firstly, the book provides reassurance when a child is developing normally. Equally, it enables you to identify those children who for some reason may not be following normative stages. Secondly, the descriptions given will help you build up a picture of a child's progress over a period of time. Thirdly, they will also enable you to anticipate, and to respond appropriately to, certain types of age-related behaviour – for example, separation anxiety. Finally, and perhaps most importantly of all, the book is an invaluable source of guidance for you in providing for a child's developmental needs.

Qualifications in child care and education

The book focuses on the areas of development defined by the leading organisations in the UK that award qualifications in child care and education, namely CACHE (Council for Awards in Children's Care and Education), City & Guilds and Edexcel/BTEC. This second edition also recognises the requirement of the new National Occupational Standards in Children's Care, Learning and Development for students to extend their knowledge and understanding of children's development from birth to the age of 16.

Every child is unique

Remember that the stages or 'milestones' of development described are *normative* indicators of development – they can only indicate general trends in development in children across the world.

There are, inevitably, some drawbacks in using normative descriptions. For example, they may cause unnecessary anxiety when a child does not achieve 'milestones' that are considered normal for a given age. Remember that the individual child's performance could be affected by a number of factors, including tiredness, anxiety or illness.

Normative assessment should always be supported by other techniques, in particular by observations; observing is an essential skill for everyone working with babies and children. At the end of each age section in the book are suggested activities which you can use to promote children's all-round development, and many of these also lend themselves to planned observations.

Reviewing development

This book also covers the current methods of reviewing development in child health clinics in the UK, and provides a useful guide to ways of stimulating development in children who have special needs. Observing children is a vital part of studying their development, and the new chapter on Theories of Child Development provides a useful link between practice and theory. A useful list of resources and a comprehensive glossary are also included.

Chapter 1

Aspects of holistic child development

It is important to keep in mind that even a tiny baby is a person. *Holistic development* sees the child in the round, as a whole person – physically, emotionally, intellectually, socially, morally, culturally and spiritually.

Learning about child development involves studying patterns of growth and development, from which guidelines for 'normal' development are drawn up.

Developmental norms are sometimes called *milestones* – they describe the recognised pattern of development that children are expected to follow. Each child will develop in a *unique* way; however, using norms helps in understanding these general patterns of development while recognising the wide variation between individuals.

Based on children and young people growing up in Western Europe, the norms described in this book show what *most* children can do at particular stages.

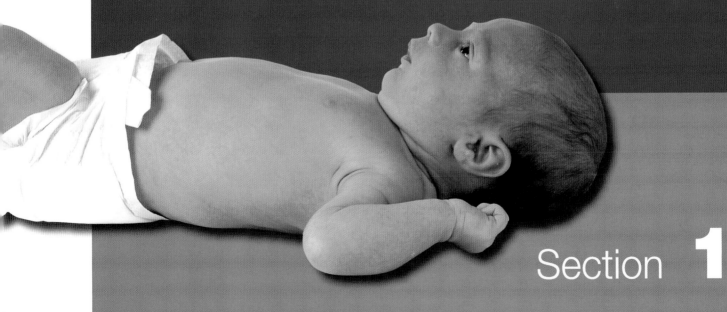

Section **1**

Areas of development

The areas of development described in this book are these:

Physical development

Physical development is the way in which the body increases in skill and becomes more complex in its performance. There are two main areas:

- **Gross motor skills:** These use the large muscles in the body, and include walking, running, climbing and the like.

- **Fine motor skills:** These include gross skills and fine skills.

  - **Gross manipulative skills** involve single limb movements, usually of the arm, for example throwing, catching and making sweeping arm movements.

  - **Fine manipulative skills** involve precise use of the hands and fingers, for example pointing, drawing, using a knife and fork or chopsticks, writing or doing up shoelaces.

▶ *Sensory development*

Physical development also includes sensory development. **Sensation** is the process by which we receive information through the senses:

- vision
- hearing
- smell
- touch
- taste
- proprioception.

Proprioception is the sense that tells people where the mobile parts of their body, such as the arms and legs, are in relation to the rest of the body.

Cognitive and language development

Cognitive or intellectual development is development of the mind – the part of the brain that is used for recognising, reasoning, knowing and understanding.

Perception involves people making sense of what they see, hear, touch, smell and taste. Perception is affected by previous experience and knowledge, and by the person's emotional state at the time.

▶ *Language development*

Language development is the development of **communication** skills. These include skills in:

- **receptive speech** – what a person understands

- **expressive speech** – the words the person produces

- **articulation** – the person's actual pronunciation of words.

Emotional and social development

▶ Emotional development

Emotional development involves the development of feelings:

- the growth of feelings about, and awareness of, *oneself*
- the development of feelings towards *other people*
- the development of **self-esteem** and a **self-concept**.

▶ Social development

Social development includes the growth of the child's relationships with other people. **Socialisation** is the process of learning the skills and attitudes that enable the child to live easily with other members of the community.

Moral and spiritual development

Moral and spiritual development consists of a developing awareness of how to relate to others ethically, morally and humanely. It involves understanding values such as honesty and respect, and acquiring **concepts** such as right and wrong and responsibility for the consequences of one's actions.

The pattern of development

Children's development follows a pattern:

▶ From simple to complex

Development progresses from simple actions to more complex ones. For example, children stand before they can walk, and walk before they can skip or hop.

▶ From head to toe

Development progresses downwards. Physical control and co-ordination begins with a child's head and develops down the body through the arms, hands and back, and finally to the legs and feet.

▶ From inner to outer

Development progresses from actions nearer the body to more complex ones further from the body. For example, children can co-ordinate their arms, using gross motor skills to reach for an object, before they have learned the fine motor skills necessary to use their fingers to pick it up.

(During **puberty** there is another growth spurt; this time the growth starts at the *outside* of the body and works *inwards*. Hands and feet expand first; the shin bones lengthen before the thigh, and the forearm before the upper arm; finally, the spine grows).

▶ *From general to specific*

Development progresses from general responses to specific ones. For example, a young baby shows pleasure by a massive general response – the eyes widen, and the legs and arms move vigorously – whereas an older child shows pleasure by smiling or using appropriate words or gestures.

The various aspects of development are intricately linked: each affects and is affected by the others. For example, once children have reached the stage of emotional development at which they feel secure when apart from their main carer, they will have access to a much wider range of relationships, experiences and opportunities for learning. Similarly, when children can use language effectively, they will have more opportunities for social interaction. If one aspect is hampered or neglected in some way, children will be challenged in reaching their full potential.

The importance of play

Play is vital to children's all-round development. Play provides opportunities for children to:

- develop confidence, self-esteem and a sense of security
- realise their potential and feel competent
- use creativity and imagination
- develop reading, thinking and problem-solving skills as well as motor skills
- learn how to control their emotions, and understand and interpret the world around them
- learn relationship and social skills, and develop values and ethics.

ICT and child development

ICT resources for young children have two distinct features; they can communicate information and/or promote interactivity.

Communicating information	Promoting interactivity
Cameras: digital still and video cameras	Computers
Audiocassettes	Musical keyboards
Television, video, DVD	Activity centres
Internet	Digital interactive TV
Mobile phones	Children's websites
Email	Remote controlled toys

The introduction of ICT in nursery settings is controversial, with both televisions and computers increasingly being used as educational tools. Some educationalists think that the best thing a very young child can do with a computer or television is to play with the box it came in. By using the box as a boat, house, car or other symbol, the child is using imagination and both initiates and remains in control of the play. Others believe that carefully selected television programmes and computer software offer children of all ages a rich learning experience, which prepares them for further use of technology.

Chapter 2

At birth

Newborn babies are already actively using all their senses to explore their new environment. They are seeing new things, listening to new sounds and smelling new odours.

When not asleep, babies are alert. Already they are learning to cope with a huge amount of new information.

Newborn babies can focus on objects less than one metre away. They show a marked preference for human faces.

They can recognise their mother's voice, and are settling into the world of noise, light, smell, taste and touch outside the womb.

Physical development

Gross motor skills

Babies:
- lie **supine** (on their backs), with the head to one side.

Other physical positions are also characteristic:

- When placed on their front (the **prone** position), babies lie with the head turned to one side, the buttocks humped up and the knees tucked under the abdomen.

- When pulled to a sitting position, the head lags

  - When held up by a hand under the chest (**ventral suspension**), the head drops below the plane of the body, and the arms and legs are partly bent (**flexion**).

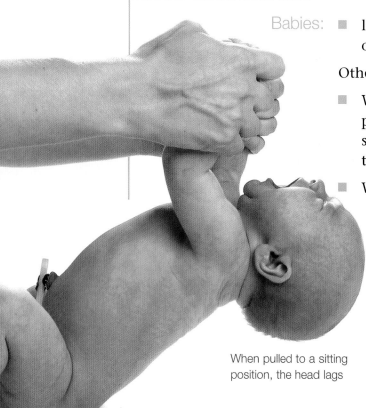

When pulled to a sitting position, the head lags

Fine motor skills

Babies:
- usually hold their hands tightly closed, but the hands may open spontaneously during feeding or when the back of the hand is stroked

- often hold their thumbs tucked in under their fingers.

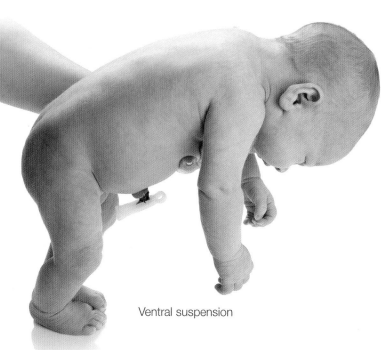

Ventral suspension

Sensory development

Babies:
- will turn their head towards the light and will stare at bright, shiny objects
- are fascinated by human faces and gaze attentively at their carer's face when being fed or cuddled
- open their eyes when held upright
- close their eyes tightly if a pencil light is shone directly into them
- like looking at high-contrast patterns and shapes
- blink in response to sound or movement
- are startled by sudden noises
- recognise their mother's or main carer's voice at less than one week old

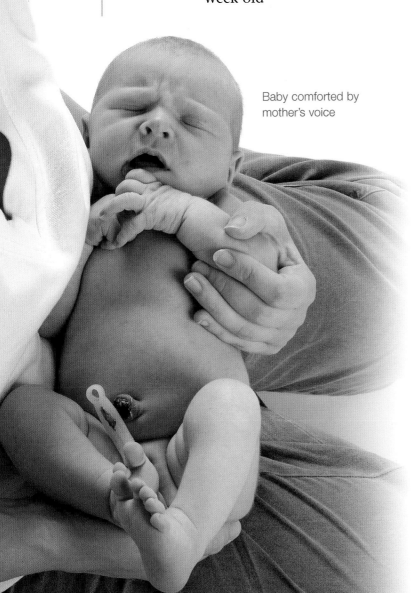

Baby comforted by mother's voice

- cannot hear very soft sounds
- if breastfed, can distinguish the smell of their mother's breasts from those of other women who are breastfeeding
- show a preference for sweet tastes over salty, sour tastes
- are sensitive to textures and to any change of position
- have sensitive skin but may not respond to a very light touch.

Reflexes of a newborn baby

Babies display a number of automatic movements, known as **primitive reflexes**, which are reflex responses to specific stimuli. These movements are inborn.

At about three months, the primitive reflexes are replaced by voluntary responses as the brain takes control of behaviour – for example, the grasp reflex has to fade before babies can learn to hold objects placed in their hands.

Primitive reflexes are important indicators of the health of the **central nervous system** of babies. If they persist beyond an expected time, this may indicate a delay in development.

▶ The swallowing and sucking reflexes

When anything is put in the mouth, babies at once suck and swallow. Some babies while still in the womb make their fingers sore by sucking them.

▶ The rooting reflex

If one side of a baby's cheek or mouth is gently touched, the baby's head turns towards the touch and the mouth purses as if in search of the nipple.

The rooting reflex

▶ The grasp reflex

When an object or a finger touches the palm of the baby's hand, the hand automatically grasps it.

The grasp reflex

The stepping or walking reflex

When held upright and tilting slightly forward, with their feet placed on a firm surface, babies will make forward stepping movements.

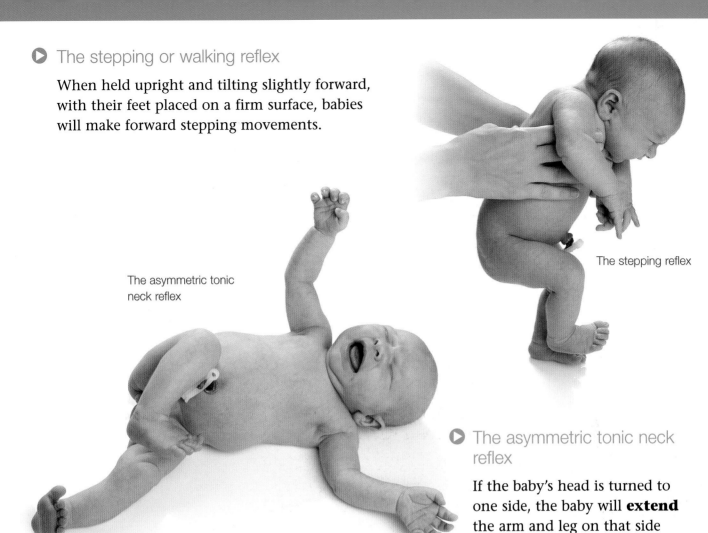

The stepping reflex

The asymmetric tonic neck reflex

The asymmetric tonic neck reflex

If the baby's head is turned to one side, the baby will **extend** the arm and leg on that side and bend the arm and leg on the opposite side.

The startle reflex

When babies are startled by a sudden loud noise or bright light, they will move their arms outwards with elbows bent and hands clenched.

The falling reflex (Moro reflex)

Any sudden movement that affects the neck gives babies the feeling that they may be dropped; they will fling out the arms and open the hands, before bringing them back over the chest as if to catch hold of something.

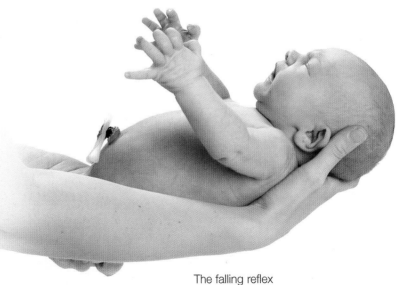

The falling reflex

Cognitive and language development

Babies:

- are beginning to develop **concepts** – concepts are abstract ideas, based on the senses and combined with growing understanding (for example, babies become aware of physical sensations such as hunger, and respond by crying)

- explore using their senses and using their own activity and movement

- make eye contact and cry to indicate need

- respond to high-pitched tones by moving their limbs

- often synchronise actions with the sound of an adult voice

- are often able to imitate, for example copying adults who open their mouth wide or stick out their tongue.

Mother and baby gazing at each other

Emotional and social development

Babies:

- use total body movements to express pleasure at bathtime or when being fed

- enjoy feeding and cuddling

- often imitate facial expressions.

Play

Newborn babies respond to things that they see, hear and feel. Play might include the following.

▶ Pulling faces

Try sticking out your tongue and opening your mouth wide – the baby may copy you.

▶ Showing objects

Try showing the baby brightly coloured woolly pompoms, balloons, shiny objects and black and white patterns. Hold the object directly in front of the baby's face, and give the baby time to focus on it. Then slowly move it.

▶ Taking turns

Talk with babies. If you talk to babies and leave time for a response, you will find that very young babies react, first with a concentrated expression and later with smiles and excited leg kicking.

Promoting development

- Provide plenty of physical contact, and maintain eye contact.
- Massage their body and limbs during or after bathing.
- Talk lovingly to babies and give them the opportunity to respond.
- Pick babies up and talk to them face to face.
- Encourage **bonding** with the baby's main carers by allowing time for them to enjoy the relationship.
- Expect no set routine within the first few weeks.
- Use bright, contrasting colours in furnishings.
- Feed babies on demand, and talk and sing to them.
- Introduce them to different household noises.
- Provide contact with other adults and children.

- Encourage babies to lie on the floor and kick and experiment safely with movement.

- Provide opportunities for them to feel the freedom of moving without a nappy or clothes on.

- Provide a mobile over the cot and/or the nappy-changing area.

- Encourage focusing and co-ordination by stringing light rattles and toys over the pram or cot.

Safely experimenting with movement

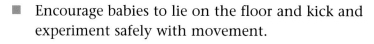

When playing with babies, always support the head – babies' neck muscles are not yet strong enough to control movement.

Never leave babies with a feeding bottle propped in their mouth.

Always place babies on their back to sleep.

Keep the temperature in a baby's room at around 20°C (68°F).

Note to parents: The safest place for your baby to sleep is in a cot in your room for the first six months.

Activities

▶ Design a mobile

Research shows that babies prefer contrasting or primary colours (not pastel shades): our brains are programmed to respond to contrasts.

1   Think of two or more designs for the mobile. (You could use a coat hanger or a cardboard tube as your basic structure.)

2   Compare your ideas, considering the following factors:

- availability of resources and materials
- skills and time required
- costs of materials
- appropriateness of the design for its purpose
- safety.

3   Select one of the designs and make the mobile.

You could use this activity in preparation for a child observation.

1   First, write down your instructions for making the mobile.

2   Now evaluate them: were they easy to follow, or did you have to modify the original plan?

3   Next, observe a baby reacting to the mobile, and record a detailed observation.

4   Did the baby react as you would expect for a baby of this age and stage of development?

▶ Contrast cards

To encourage visual development, make some cards with different black and white patterns.

Attach the cards securely to the inside of the baby's pram or cot.

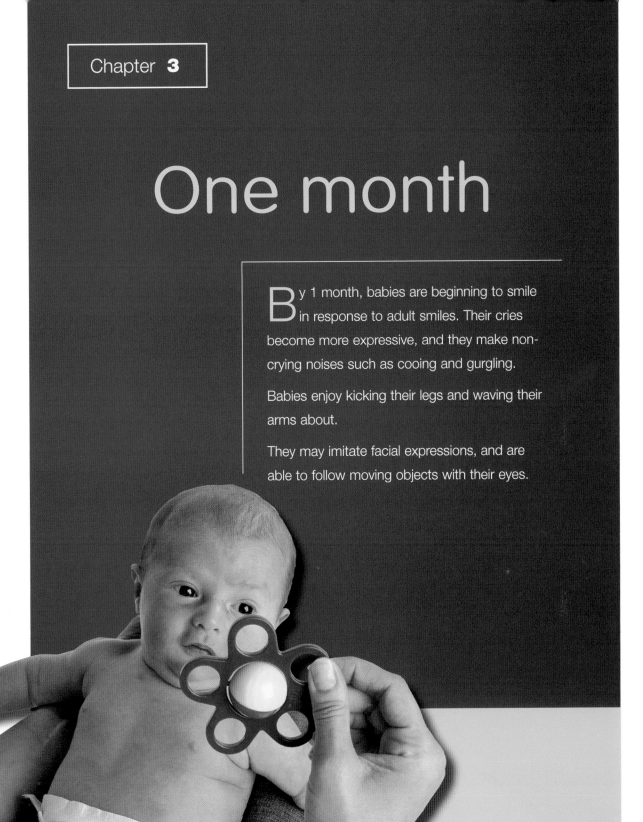

Chapter **3**

One month

By 1 month, babies are beginning to smile in response to adult smiles. Their cries become more expressive, and they make non-crying noises such as cooing and gurgling.

Babies enjoy kicking their legs and waving their arms about.

They may imitate facial expressions, and are able to follow moving objects with their eyes.

Physical development

Gross motor skills

Babies:

- keep their head to one side when lying on their back (supine), with the arm and the leg on the face side outstretched, the knees apart, and the soles of the feet turned inwards

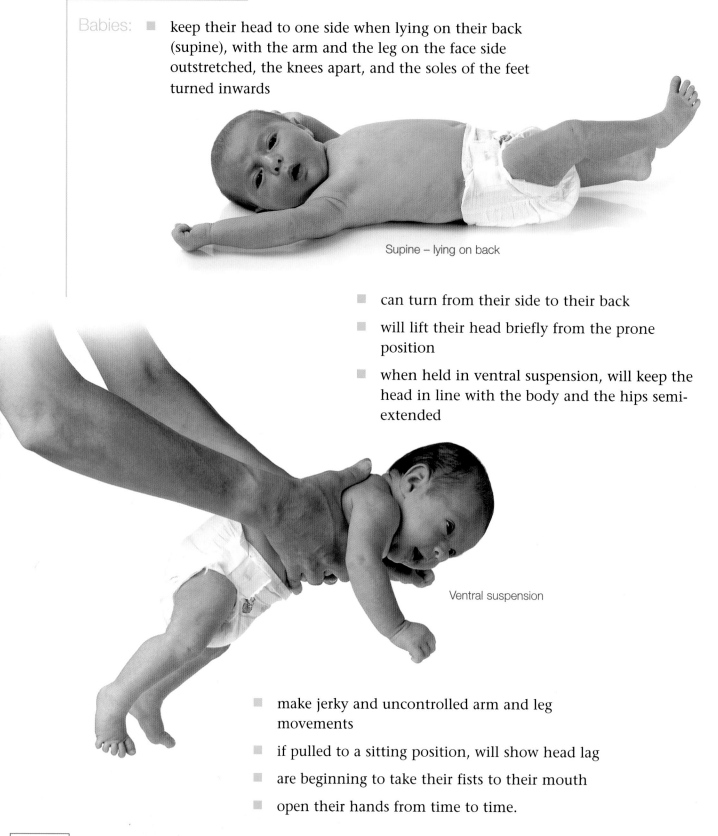

Supine – lying on back

- can turn from their side to their back
- will lift their head briefly from the prone position
- when held in ventral suspension, will keep the head in line with the body and the hips semi-extended

Ventral suspension

- make jerky and uncontrolled arm and leg movements
- if pulled to a sitting position, will show head lag
- are beginning to take their fists to their mouth
- open their hands from time to time.

Fine motor skills

Babies:
- show interest and excitement by their facial expressions
- open their hands to grasp an adult's finger.

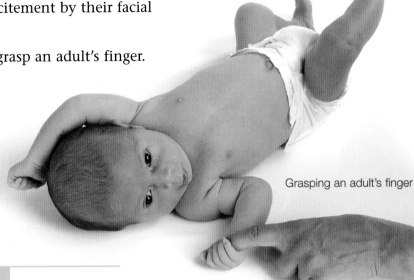

Grasping an adult's finger

Sensory development

Babies:
- focus their gaze at 20–25 cm (8–10 inches)
- turn their head towards a diffuse light source, and stare at bright, shiny objects
- may move their head towards the source of a sound, but are not yet able to locate the sound
- are startled by sudden noises – when hearing a particular sound, they may momentarily 'freeze'
- blink defensively when something comes towards them
- follow the movement of a bright, dangling toy moved slowly in their line of vision – this is known as **tracking**.

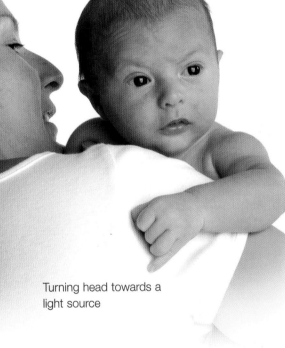

Turning head towards a light source

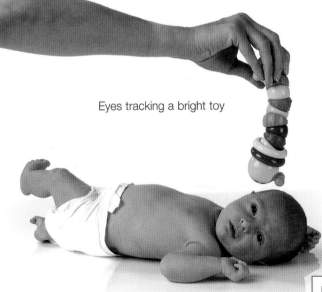

Eyes tracking a bright toy

Cognitive and language development

Babies:

- recognise their primary carers and show this by responding to them with a combination of excited movements, coos and smiles

- begin to repeat enjoyable movements, such as thumb-sucking

- make non-crying noises, such as cooing and gurgling

- cry in more expressive ways

- interact with an adult holding them up face-to-face, by simultaneously looking, listening, vocalising, and moving their arms and legs excitedly.

Emotional and social development

Babies:

- smile in response to an adult

- gaze attentively at the adult's face when being fed

- are beginning to show a particular **temperament** – for example, placid or excitable

- enjoy sucking

- turn to regard a nearby speaker's face.

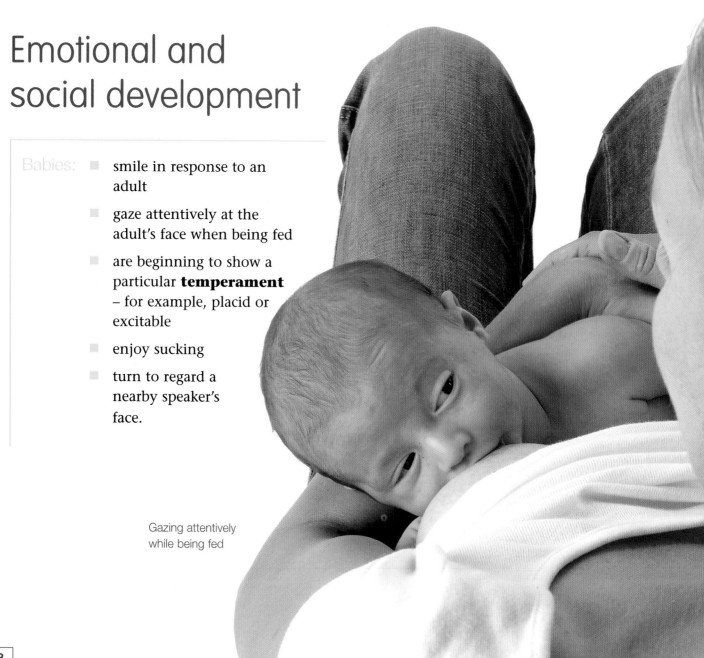

Gazing attentively while being fed

Play

Babies:
- love to watch movement such as trees in the wind, or moving bright, contrasting objects placed within their field of vision
- enjoy listening to the sound of bells, music and voices, and to rhythmic sounds.

Promoting development

- Use a special supporting infant chair so that babies can see adult activity.
- Let them kick freely without a nappy on.
- Gently massage the baby's body and limbs during or after bathing.
- Use brightly coloured mobiles and wind chimes over the baby's cot and/or changing mat.
- Encourage focusing and co-ordination by hanging light rattles and toys over the pram or cot.
- Talk to and smile with the baby.
- Sing while feeding or bathing the baby. Allow time for the baby to respond.
- Learn to differentiate between the baby's cries, and to respond to them appropriately.
- Encourage laughter by tickling the baby.
- Hold the baby close to promote a feeling of security.
- Try tying a few small bells safely around the baby's wrists. This encourages babies to watch their hands.

SafetyPoints

Never leave rattles or similar toys in a baby's cot or pram. They could become wedged in the baby's mouth and might cause suffocation.

Do not leave a baby unattended on a table, work surface, bed or sofa. Lie the baby on the floor instead.

Activities

▶ Following movement

At around 6–10 weeks, babies begin to follow movement with their eyes. One way of promoting visual development -- and of improving head–eye co-ordination – in young babies is to let them watch a moving toy.

1   Select a favourite toy – perhaps a teddy or a brightly coloured toy.

2   Hold the toy about 1 metre (3 feet) in front of the baby.

3   Slowly move the toy from side to side so that the baby's eyes can follow it.

4   As the baby gets better at following the movement, swing the toy further each way.

5   Try different directions – up and down, towards and away from the baby.

▶ Baby massage

Massage has many benefits for a baby. It is very soothing and can calm a fretful baby. It is also a very good way of showing love. Parental permission should always be obtained before undertaking baby massage.

The main points to remember are that the experience should:

- benefit both the baby and the carer, creating a feeling of calm and increasing the carer's confidence in handling techniques
- be conducted in a relaxed atmosphere, avoiding distractions such as the telephone or other people
- be carried out using very gentle strokes
- always be symmetrical – both sides of the baby's body should be massaged at the same time
- take place in a warm room
- be an unhurried, relaxing experience.

The following is an appropriate massage sequence.

1   Prepare the room by making sure that there are no draughts and that the room is warm. Remove any jewellery and make sure that your nails have no rough edges.

2   You could use a mat with a thick towel on the floor, or simply lie the baby along your lap – make sure your own back is supported.

3   Use a baby oil. Warm it by first rubbing it between your palms.

4   Work down from the baby's head, using a light, circular motion. First massage the crown of the baby's head *very gently*; then move on to the forehead, cheeks and ears.

5   Gently massage the baby's neck, from the ears down to the shoulders, and from the chin to the chest.

6   Gently stroke the baby's arms, starting from the shoulders and going all the way to the fingertips.

7   Stroke down the baby's chest and tummy, rubbing in a circular direction.

8   Gently massage the baby's legs, from the thighs to the ankles.

9   Massage the baby's feet, stroking from heel to toe. Concentrate on each toe individually.

10 Finally, turn the baby over onto the front and gently massage the back.

Throughout the procedure, talk softly to the baby and always leave one hand in contact with the baby's body, to provide security and comfort. Always ensure you obtain a parent's permission before undertaking baby massage.

(See also *Baby Massage*, Heinemann)

Chapter 4

Three months

By 3 months, babies are showing more interest in playthings.

They like to kick vigorously and to clasp their hands together.

They respond to familiar situations with a combination of excited movements, smiles and a variety of vocalisations, such as cries, cooing sounds and chuckles.

Physical development

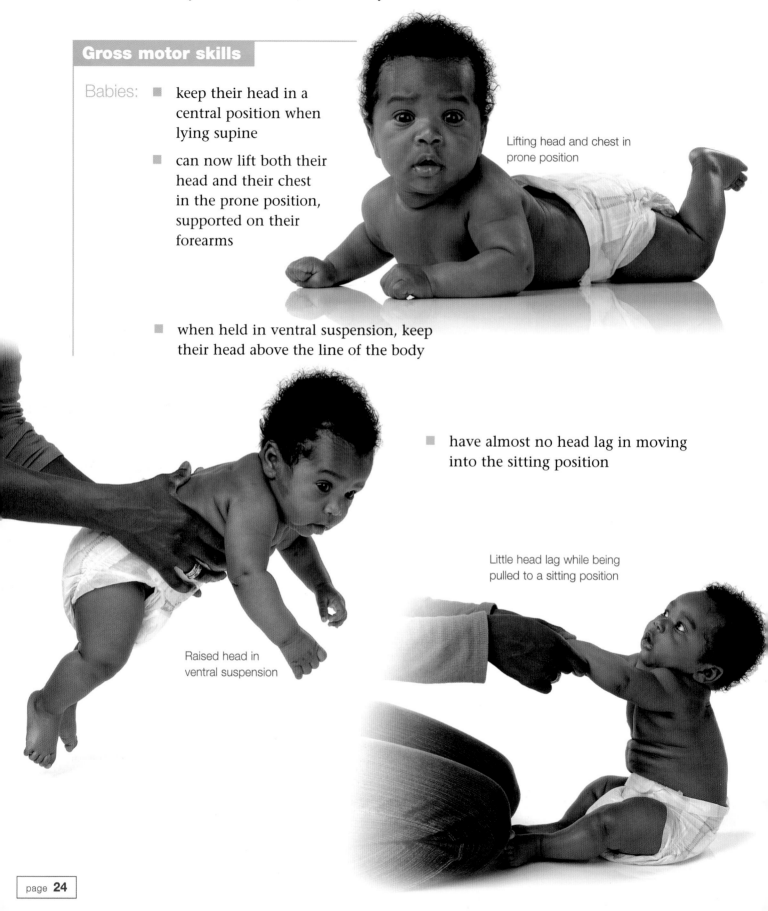

Gross motor skills

Babies:

- keep their head in a central position when lying supine

- can now lift both their head and their chest in the prone position, supported on their forearms

Lifting head and chest in prone position

- when held in ventral suspension, keep their head above the line of the body

- have almost no head lag in moving into the sitting position

Little head lag while being pulled to a sitting position

Raised head in ventral suspension

- when held, can sit with their back straight
- kick vigorously, with their legs alternating or occasionally together
- can wave their arms and bring their hands together over their body.

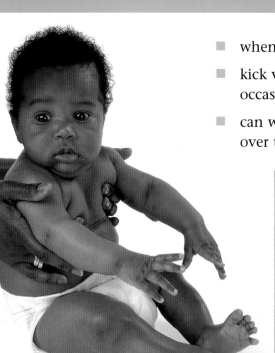

Straight back when sitting

Fine motor skills

Babies:
- move their head to follow adults' movements
- watch their hands and play with their fingers

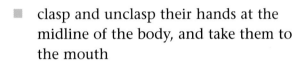

Taking the hand to the mouth

- clasp and unclasp their hands at the midline of the body, and take them to the mouth
- can hold a rattle for a brief time before dropping it.

Sensory development

Babies:
- are able to focus their eyes on the same point
- can move their head deliberately to gaze around them
- prefer moving objects to still ones – their eyes will follow a moving toy from side to side (through 180°)

Eyes following a moving toy

- turn their eyes towards a sound source, especially a human voice
- respond to their name being called
- often suck their lips in response to the sounds of food preparation
- are distressed by sudden loud noises
- are fascinated by human faces and can recognise their mother's or main carer's face in a photograph.

Cognitive and language development

Babies:
- take an increasing interest in their surroundings
- laugh and vocalise, with increasing tone and intensity
- are becoming conversational by cooing, gurgling and chuckling – they can exchange coos with a familiar person
- smile in response to speech
- show an increasing interest in playthings
- cry loudly when expressing a need
- understand cause and effect – for example, they will deliberately shake a rattle, knowing that it will make a noise.

Emotional and social development

Babies:
- show enjoyment at caring routines such as bathtime
- fix their eyes unblinkingly on the carer's face when feeding
- respond with obvious pleasure to loving attention and cuddles

- stay awake for longer periods of time (70 per cent of babies at this age sleep through the night)

- smile at familiar people and at strangers.

Play

Babies:
- enjoy holding rattles, chiming balls and musical toys

- love to explore different textures, for example on an activity mat.

Responding with pleasure to being cuddled

Promoting development

- Use a supporting infant chair so that the baby can watch adult activity.

- Provide brightly coloured mobiles and wind chimes to encourage focusing at 20 cm (8 inches).

- Place some toys on a blanket or play mat on the floor. Let the baby lie on her or his tummy to play with the toys for short periods.

- Give the baby a rattle to hold.

- Attach objects above the cot that make a noise when touched.

- Imitate the sounds made by the baby and encourage repetition.

- Sing nursery rhymes.

- Change the baby's position frequently so that there are different things to look at and to experience.

- Encourage contact with other adults and children.

- Try action rhymes with the baby on your lap, such as 'This little piggy went to market …'.

- Respond to the baby's needs and show enjoyment in providing care.

- Tickle the baby to provide enjoyment.

- Massage or stroke the baby's limbs when bathing or if using massage oil.

SafetyPoints

Always protect babies, of *all* skin tones, from exposure to sunlight. Use a special sun-protection cream, a sun hat to protect the face and neck, and a pram canopy.

Never leave small objects within reach – everything finds its way to a baby's mouth.

When you buy goods, always check for an appropriate safety symbol.

Activities

▶ A simple game or toy

Design and make a simple game or toy that will encourage a baby's sensory development.

1   Think about the stage of development the child has reached. Plan to make a game or toy that will promote development of one or more of the baby's senses – examples are an activity mat, sound lotto, a 'feely' bag, or a game of matching smells.

2   Points to consider are:
  ● safety
  ● hygiene
  ● suitability for the purpose.

You could use this activity for a child observation.

1   First, say which sense you hope your game or toy will develop, and describe how it will help.

2   Next, observe a baby playing with the game or toy, and record a detailed observation.

3   Did the baby react as you would expect for a baby of this age and stage of development?

▶ A secret mirror table

Mirrors are a good way to promote visual awareness: they catch the light and reflect different colours, and babies can also see their own movements reflected.

1   Stick a few mirror tiles securely to the underside of a low table.

2   Place the baby underneath the table so that she or he can look up into the mirror tiles. Check that there is enough light.

3   Try to provide a contrasting image – for instance, if the baby's clothing is pale, place the baby on a dark sheet.

SafetyPoints

Before placing the baby on the floor, make sure that there are no draughts.

Chapter 5

Six months

By 6 months, babies are able to reach for and grab things with both hands. They extend their exploration by using their hands to touch, stroke and pat. Most toys are transferred to the mouth.

They love to imitate sounds and enjoy babbling.

They continue to find other people fascinating, but are wary of strangers.

Physical development

Babies:
- if lying on their back can roll over onto their stomach

- if lying on their stomach can lift their head and chest, supporting themselves on their arms and hands

- can use their shoulders to pull themselves into a sitting position

Using the hands and arms for support

Using the shoulders while moving to a sitting position

- can bear almost all their own weight

- when held standing, do so with a straight back

- when held sitting, do so with a straight back

Bearing most of the weight

Sitting with a straight back

- when held on the floor, bounce their feet up and down
- lift their legs into a vertical position and grasp one or both feet with their hands

Grasping a foot with the hands

- kick vigorously with their legs alternating
- move their arms purposefully and hold them up, indicating a wish to be lifted
- change the angle of their body to reach out for an object.

Fine motor skills

Babies:
- reach and grab when a small toy is offered
- use their whole hand (**palmar grasp**) to pass a toy from one hand to the other

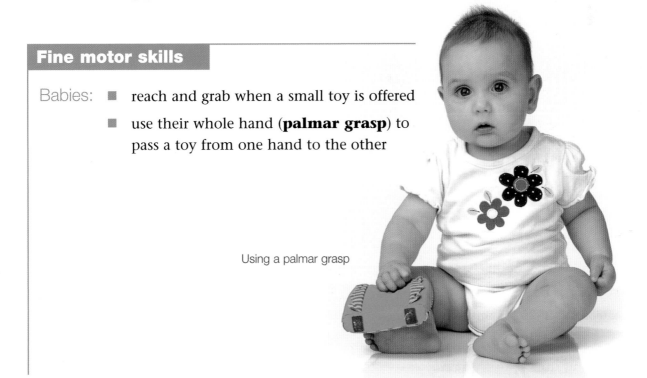

Using a palmar grasp

- poke at small objects with their index finger
- explore objects by putting them in their mouth.

Exploring objects with the mouth

Sensory development

Babies:
- adjust their position to see objects
- are visually very alert, and follow another child's or an adult's activities across the room with increased alertness
- turn towards the source when they hear sounds at ear level.

Cognitive and language development

Babies:
- understand the meaning of words such as 'bye-bye', 'mama' or 'dada'
- understand objects and know what to expect of them – given a can that makes a noise, for instance, they will test it for other unexpected behaviour
- turn immediately when they hear mother's or main carer's voice at a distance
- show some understanding of the emotional state of their mother's or main carer's voice
- understand 'up' and 'down' and make appropriate gestures, such as raising their arms to be picked up
- babble spontaneously, using first monosyllables such as 'ga, ga' and then double syllables such as 'goo-ga', and later combining more syllables
- talk to themselves in a tuneful, sing-song voice
- squeal with delight.

Emotional and social development

Babies:
- manage to feed themselves using their fingers
- offer toys to others
- are more wary of strangers
- show distress when their mother leaves
- are more aware of other people's feelings, crying if a sibling cries, for example, or laughing when others do – this is called *recognising an emotion*; it does not mean that they are *really* feeling that emotion.

Play

Babies:
- show delight in response to active play

Delighting in active play

- enjoy playing with stacking beakers and bricks
- love to explore objects with both their hands and their mouth
- play with a rolling ball when in a sitting position.

Promoting development

- Encourage confidence and balance by placing toys around the sitting baby.

- Provide rattles and toys that can be hung over the cot – these encourage the baby to reach and grab.

- Encourage mobility by placing toys just out of the baby's reach.

- Provide toys that babies may safely transfer to their mouth.

- Build a tower of bricks with the baby, and share the delight when it topples over.

- Look at picture books together.

- Encourage the baby to point at objects with you.

- Talk about everyday things.

- Widen the baby's experience, for example by going on outings that include animals.

- Imitate animal sounds and encourage the baby to copy you.

- Allow plenty of time for play. Provide simple musical instruments such as a xylophone or a wooden spoon and saucepan.

- Use a mirror to develop the baby's recognition of herself or himself.

- Provide suction toys on tabletops.

- Sing nursery rhymes and lullabies.

- Provide cardboard boxes that the baby can put things into and take things out of.

Looking at a picture book together

Make sure that all furniture is stable and has no sharp corners.

Always supervise a baby when trying 'finger foods' or at mealtimes.

Always supervise water play.

Activities

▶ Action rhymes

Action rhymes promote memory and listening skills. Babies quickly learn to anticipate the next phrase of the rhyme and its associated action.

Two popular rhymes to try with a young baby are 'This Little Piggy' and 'Pat-a-Cake'.

1 'This Little Piggy'

This little piggy went to market

This little piggy stayed at home

This little piggy had roast beef

This little piggy had none

And this little piggy
Went wee wee wee I can't find my way home.

Count the first five lines of the rhyme on the baby's toes, then on the last line run your hand up the baby's leg to tickle her or his tummy.

2 'Pat-a-Cake'

Pat-a-cake, pat-a-cake, baker's man

Bake me a cake as fast as you can

Pat it and prick it and mark it with 'B'

And put it in the oven for baby and me.

Clap your hands in time to the rhythm of the song and encourage the baby to clap along with you.

▶ Taking turns

Try a simple game of give-and-take with the baby. This will encourage the skill of being able to 'let go' of an object, as well as promoting the concept of turn-taking.

The following is just one way of doing this:

1 Seat the baby safely, supported by cushions or in a high chair.

2 Pass the baby a toy that can be grasped with both hands, such as a soft ball or a rattle.

3 Ask the baby: 'Please give me the toy' – or 'ball', or whatever it is – and hold out your hands to receive it.

4 Then pass the toy back to the baby, saying: 'You can have it back now – here you are.'

Throughout the game, encourage the baby to pass the object from one hand to another – by showing how you do this – before passing it to you. This will increase her or his manipulative skills.

Chapter 6

Nine months

Babies enjoy exploring their environment by crawling or shuffling on their bottoms.

They often bounce in time to music and take pleasure in songs and action rhymes. They can sit, lean forward and pull objects towards them.

Babies understand their daily routine and like to imitate adult speech and gestures.

Physical development

Gross motor skills

Babies:
- can maintain a sitting position with a straight back

- can sit unsupported for up to 15 minutes

- turn their body to look sideways when stretching out to pick up a toy from the floor

- pull themselves to a standing position, but are unable to lower themselves and tend to fall backwards with a bump

- stand holding on to furniture

- find ways of moving about the floor – for example, by rolling, wriggling, or crawling on their stomach

- may take some steps when both hands are held.

Sitting alone playing with toy

Attempting to crawl

Grasping an object using a pincer grip

Fine motor skills

Babies:
- manipulate toys by passing them from one hand to the other

- can grasp objects between finger and thumb in a **pincer grasp**

- can release a toy from their grasp by dropping it, but cannot yet put it down voluntarily

- move arms up and down together when excited.

Cognitive and language development

Babies:
- can judge the size of an object up to 60 cm (2 feet) away

- look in the correct direction for fallen toys

- watch a toy being hidden and then look for it – this shows that they know that an object can exist even when it is no longer in sight (**object permanence**)

Hiding an object…

…looking for it

…and 'finding' it again

- recognise familiar pictures

- understand their daily routine and will follow simple instructions such as 'kiss teddy'

- use an increasing variety of intonation when babbling

- enjoy communicating with sounds

- imitate adult sounds, like a cough or a 'brrr' noise

- understand and obey the command 'no'

- know general characteristics of their language – they will not respond to a foreign language.

Emotional and social development

Babies:
- enjoy songs and action rhymes
- still prefer to be near to a familiar adult
- play alone for long periods
- show definite likes and dislikes at meals and at bedtimes
- often need to have a **comfort object**, such as a blanket or a favourite teddy
- still take everything to the mouth

Taking objects to the mouth

- may drink from a cup with help
- enjoy pointing at objects
- enjoy making noises by banging toys.

Play

Babies:
- play alone for long periods
- enjoy making noises by banging toys
- like to play with empty cardboard boxes.

Playing alone

Promoting development

- Allow plenty of time for play.

- Encourage mobility by placing toys just out of reach.

- Provide small objects for babies to pick up – choose objects that are safe when chewed, such as pieces of biscuit – but always supervise them.

- Provide bath toys such as beakers, sponges and funnels.

- Provide picture books for babies to explore.

Exploring a picture book

- Provide stacking and nesting toys.

- Play peek-a-boo games, and hide-and-seek.

- Roll balls for the baby to bring back to you.

- Encourage self-feeding and tolerate messes.

- Talk constantly to babies, and continue with rhymes and action songs.

Chapter 6 Nine months

SafetyPoints

Always supervise eating and drinking. Never leave babies alone with finger foods such as bananas, carrots or cheese.

Use childproof containers for tablets and vitamins. Ensure that the containers are closed properly.

Use a locked cupboard for storing dangerous household chemicals such as bleach, disinfectant and white spirit.

Activities

1   Choose one of the baby's favourite playthings – perhaps a small soft toy or rattle.

2   Place the baby in a sitting position or lying on his or her stomach.

3   While the baby is watching, place the toy in full view and within easy reach. The baby may reach for the object.

4   Still in full view of the baby, partly cover the toy with a cloth so that only part of it is visible. Again, the baby may reach for the toy.

5   While the baby is reaching for the toy, cover the toy completely with the cloth. Does the baby continue to reach for it?

6   While the baby is still interested in the toy, and again in full view of the baby, completely cover the toy with the cloth once more. Notice whether the baby tries to pull the cloth away or to search for the toy in some way.

Games of hide-and-seek indicate whether the baby has developed the concept of **object permanence**. You could explore this in a child observation. You will need to find a baby aged between six months and a year whose parent is happy for you to try this activity.

1   Follow the procedure outlined above. At each stage, note whether the baby reaches for the toy.

2   Write up the results of the activity in the form of an observation.

3   If possible, compare this observation with observations of other children.

Research shows that **step 4** – continuing to reach for the partly covered toy – is typically experienced at about six months; **step 5** at about seven months; and **step 6** at about eight months.

Twelve months

The way babies view their world changes dramatically as they become more mobile, crawling rapidly or cruising along and using the furniture for support.

At 12 months they are usually still shy with strangers. Often they have a favourite comfort object, such as a teddy or a cloth.

Language develops into conversation, with increasing intonation, although there are very few recognisable words.

They are developing their own sense of identity.

Physical development

Gross motor skills

Babies:

- can rise to a sitting position from lying down

- can rise to standing without help from furniture or people

- can stand alone for a few moments

- can crawl on their hands and knees, bottom-shuffle, or use their hands and feet to move rapidly about the floor ('bear-walking')

- can 'cruise' along using furniture as a support

- can probably walk alone, with their feet wide apart and their arms raised to maintain balance – or walk with one hand held.

Walking with one hand held

Walking alone, with feet apart

By 13 months, babies:

- can often walk (about 50 per cent of babies walk by this age), but tend to fall over frequently and sit down rather suddenly.

By 15 months, babies:

- crawl upstairs safely and may come downstairs backwards

- are generally able to walk alone

- kneel without support.

Fine motor skills

Babies:

- can pick up small objects with a fine pincer grasp, between the thumb and the tip of the index finger

- can point with the index finger at objects of interest

- can release a small object into someone's hand

- can hold a crayon in a palmar grasp, and turn several pages of a book at once

- show a preference for one hand over the other, but use either

- drop and throw toys deliberately – and look to see where they have fallen

- build with a few bricks and arrange toys on the floor.

Showing a preference for one hand over the other

By 15 months, babies:

- can put small objects into a bottle

- can grasp a crayon with either hand in a palmar grasp, and imitate to-and-fro scribble

- may build a tower of two cubes after this has been demonstrated.

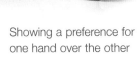

Sensory development

Babies:

- can see almost as well as an adult – their visual memory is very good: they may find things that an adult has mislaid

- know and respond immediately to their own name, and recognise familiar sounds and voices

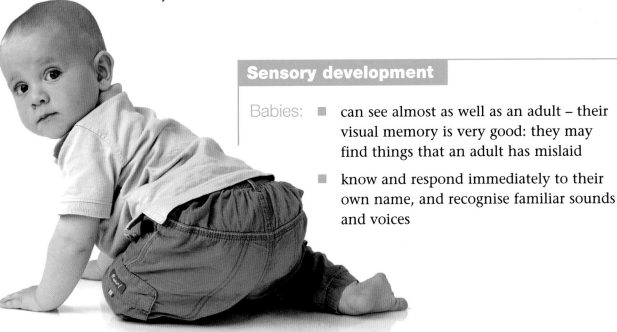

Turning in response to his own name

- stroke, pat and turn objects in their hands, and recognise familiar objects by touch alone
- discriminate between different foods by taste, and show a preference for sweet, salty and fatty flavours
- often enjoy watching television.

By 15 months, babies:

- demand objects out of reach by pointing with their index finger
- point to familiar people, animals or toys when requested.

Cognitive and language development

Babies:
- use trial-and-error methods to learn about objects
- understand simple instructions associated with a gesture, such as 'come to Daddy', 'clap hands', and 'wave bye-bye'
- both point and look to where others point, which implies some understanding of how others see and think
- speak two to six or more recognisable words and show that they understand many more – babbling has developed into a much more speech-like form, with increased intonation
- hand objects to adults when asked, and begin to treat objects in an appropriate way, for example cuddle a teddy but use a hairbrush.

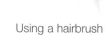

Using a hairbrush

Deaf babies stop babbling at around the age of 12 months because they begin to learn the special manual gestures of sign language.

By 15 months, babies:

- understand the names of various parts of the body
- identify pictures of a few named objects

- understand 'no', 'show me' and 'look'
- watch where objects fall, and can seek out a hidden toy
- move one object to reach another that was hidden from view.

Seeing a toy and a beaker together...

...recognising that the hidden toy may be with the beaker...

...and finding the toy

Emotional and social development

Babies:
- are emotionally **labile** – that is, they are likely to have fluctuating moods
- are closely dependent upon an adult's reassuring presence
- often want a comfort object, such as a teddy or a piece of cloth
- are still shy with strangers
- are affectionate towards familiar people
- enjoy socialising at mealtimes, joining in conversations while mastering the task of self-feeding
- help with daily routines, such as getting washed and dressed
- play pat-a-cake and wave goodbye, both spontaneously and on request.

By 15 months, babies:
- repeatedly throw objects to the floor in play or rejection (this is known as **casting**)
- carry dolls or teddies by their limbs, hair or clothing.

Play

Babies:
- enjoy playing with bricks, and with containers – they put toys into them and then take them out
- love to play with toys that they can move along with their feet
- enjoy looking at picture books.

Promoting development

- Provide a wheeled push-and-pull toy to promote confidence in walking.
- Provide stacking toys and bricks.
- Read picture books with simple rhymes.

- Arrange a corner of the kitchen or garden for messy play. Encourage the use of water, play dough or paint.

- Encourage skills of **creativity** by providing thick crayons and paint brushes and large sheets of paper (such as wall lining paper).

- Play simple games with the baby that involve action and taking turns, such as the 'hand sandwich' game.

Playing with a truck that is also a container

- Join in games of 'let's pretend' to encourage skills of **imagination** – for example, pretending to be animals or to drive a bus.

- Encourage **role-play** games of make-believe – for example, pretending to be a doctor, a vet or a superhero.

- Talk to the baby about everyday activities, but always allow time for a response.

- Provide an interesting, varied environment, which contains pictures, music, books and food, all of which stimulate the senses.

- Consider attending a mother-and-toddler group or a similar group.

SafetyPoints

As babies become more mobile, you need to be vigilant at all times. This is a very high-risk age for accidents.

Always supervise sand and water play.

Use safety equipment such as safety catches for cupboards and stair gates, ideally at the top and bottom of stairs.

Activities

▶ A pull-along snake

Once a child is walking with confidence, you could make a colourful pull-along toy. Brightly painted cotton reels threaded onto soft cord or string make an attractive 'snake' for children to pull along. Alternatively, you could thread together plastic hair rollers or large round beads.

1   Paint 10–12 large cotton reels in bright colours, using lead-free paint.

2   Thread the reels onto a cord, about 0.75 m (20 inches) long.

3   Knot the cord to ensure that the reels are about 0.5 cm (¼ inch) apart, so that the snake will twist and turn when pulled.

4   Use a large oval bead to make the snake's head. Paint an eye on each side.

5   Use small wooden or plastic beads to make an easy-to-grip handle.

This activity promotes the motor skills of balance and co-ordination, and encourages children to become aware of their ability to control their own environment.

▶ Choosing toys for babies

Visit a toyshop and look at the range of toys for babies under 18 months old. Make a list – you could group the toys and activities under two headings:

■   toys that will strengthen muscles and improve co-ordination skills

■   toys that will particularly stimulate the senses of touch, hearing and sight.

Check the safety symbols shown on the toys.

If you were asked to suggest toys and activities for a baby with visual impairment, what specific toys could you suggest? Why?

Nutrition guidelines for healthy growth and development

The first year

In the first few months of life, babies will get all the nutrients they require from breast or formula milk. Solid foods are gradually introduced at around 4–6 months; this is called **weaning**. The chart below gives some ideas for introducing solid foods to babies at different stages:

4 to 6 months	6 to 8 months	9 to 12 months
Baby rice mixed with breast or formula milk. Puréed vegetables and fruit: e.g. carrots, potato, apple. Thin porridge made from oat or rice flakes or cornmeal. Finely puréed dhal or lentils.	Coarser minces or purées of vegetables, chicken, meat, fish or lentils and pulses like aduki beans. Lumpier finger foods: e.g. chopped hard-boiled egg yolk, cubed or grated hard cheese, pasta, raw soft fruit and vegetables, e.g. tomato, banana. Some wheat-based breakfast cereals and bread.	Wholemeal breads, cereals and pasta. Chopped meats, chicken, fish and liver. Pieces of cheese. Lightly cooked or raw vegetables and fruits. Adult textures for potatoes, noodles, and puddings, e.g. rice pudding. Yoghurt or fromage frais. Unsweetened orange juice as a drink with meals.
Foods to avoid		
Cows' milk: only use breast or formula milk to liquefy food. Citrus fruit & soft summer fruits. Wheat (cereals, flour, bread) Spinach, turnip, beetroot. Eggs Nuts Salty, fatty and sugary foods	Cows' milk, except in very small quantities Chillies or chilli powder Egg whites Nuts Sugar Salt Fatty foods Fizzy drinks	Foods meant for adults, such as gravies or sauces – as these may be high in salt and additives Whole nuts Salt Sugar Fatty food
From one year onwards		
Offer any food that is wholesome and that the child can swallow. Babies can have small portions of family meals. Take the baby's portion out before adding salt, leave as adult texture, and chop to bite size if needed. Whole (full fat) milk as a drink and soft cheeses. Lean meat and oily fish, e.g. sardines, kippers.		

Chapter **7** Twelve months

Chapter 8

Eighteen months

Children of 18 months enjoy being able to walk well and can climb up and down stairs with help.

They can pick up small objects with a delicate pincer grasp, and show a preference for using one hand.

They enjoy simple picture books, and can understand and obey simple commands.

Children have an increasing desire for independence, and are developing a recognisable character and **personality** of their own.

Physical development

Children:
- can walk steadily and stop safely, without sitting down suddenly

Walking steadily – even while carrying toy

Climbing onto an adult chair…

Squatting to pick something up

…and turning around to sit on it

- can climb forward into an adult chair and then turn around and sit
- can kneel upright without support
- can squat to pick up or move a toy
- can move without support from a squatting position to standing

- can climb up and down stairs if their hand is held or using a rail for balance – they put two feet on each step before moving on to the next step
- can crawl backwards (on the stomach) down stairs alone
- can run steadily but are unable to avoid obstacles in their path.

Moving from squatting to standing

Fine motor skills: gross manipulative skills

Children:
- can point to known objects
- can build a tower of three or more bricks.

Fine motor skills: fine manipulative skills

Children:
- can use a delicate pincer grasp to pick up very small objects
- can use a spoon when feeding themselves
- can hold a pencil in their whole hand or between the thumb and the first two fingers (this is called the **primitive tripod grasp**)

- can scribble to and fro with a pencil
- can thread large beads onto a lace or string
- can control their wrist movement to manipulate objects
- can remove small objects from a bottle by turning it upside-down.

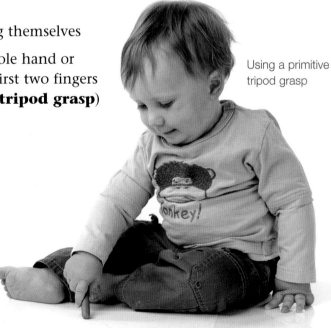

Using a primitive tripod grasp

Children:
- recognise familiar people at a distance
- realise that they are looking at themselves in the mirror
- no longer take everything to their mouths to explore it.

Cognitive and language development

Children:
- know the names of parts of their bodies, and can point to them when asked
- use 6–40 recognisable words and understand many more (the word most often used is 'no'!)
- echo the last part of what others say (**echolalia**)
- over-extend words or signs, giving them several meanings (**holophrase**) – for example, 'cat' may be used to refer to *all* animals, not just cats
- begin waving their arms up and down, meaning 'Start again', 'More' or 'I like it'
- use **gestures** alongside words
- indicate desire by pointing, urgent vocalisations or words
- obey simple instructions such as 'Shut the door', and respond to simple questions such as 'Where's the pussy-cat?'
- enjoy trying to sing, as well as listening to songs and rhymes
- refer to themselves by name
- recognise that people may have different desires (younger babies assume that everyone feels the same as they do).

Emotional and social development

Playing contentedly alone

Children:
- remember where objects belong (this reflects an increase in long-term memory)
- play contentedly alone (**solitary play**), but *prefer* to be near a familiar adult or sibling
- are eager to be independent, for example to dress themselves ('Me do it!')
- are aware that others are fearful or anxious for them as they climb on or off chairs etc.
- alternate between clinging and resistance
- may easily become frustrated, with occasional temper tantrums
- may indicate toilet needs by restlessness or words
- can follow and enjoy stories and rhymes that include repetition.

Play

Children:
- like things that screw and unscrew
- enjoy posting objects into boxes, as when posting letters
- like paints and crayons
- enjoy sand and water play, and associated toys
- like to play matching and sorting games, for example stacking beakers
- enjoy simple jigsaw puzzles
- love puppet play and action rhymes.

Playing with a glove puppet

Promoting development

Identifying details in a book

- Continue to provide walker trucks, pull-along animals and the like.
- Encourage play with messy materials, such as sand, water and play dough.
- Provide low, stable furniture to climb on.
- Provide pop-up toys, stacking toys and hammer-and-peg toys, which develop hand–eye co-ordination skills.
- Provide balls to roll, kick or throw.
- Provide toys that encourage make-believe play and language skills, such as simple puppets, dressing-up clothes or toy telephones.

- Use action rhymes and singing games to promote conversation and confidence. Play with other children will help, too.
- Provide bath toys, such as simple beakers, sprinkling toys and waterproof books.
- Use finger-paints and wax crayons to encourage creative skills.
- Provide picture books, and encourage children to turn the pages and to identify details in the pictures.

SafetyPoints

Always supervise children in the bath. Never leave a child alone in the bath, even for a few minutes.

When children are climbing or playing outside, be aware of dangers such as sharp objects, litter or unfenced ponds.

Activities

▶ A treasure basket

Make a treasure basket for a child aged 18 months.

1. Use a strong, shallow cardboard box, an old solid wooden drawer or a wicker basket.

2. Check that there are no staples, splinters or jagged edges.

3. Select a variety of interesting objects (about 10–15 in all) that will stimulate each of the child's senses – objects with different shapes, weights, colours and textures. You may also be able to include objects that have a distinctive smell, such as a small empty perfume bottle or a lavender bag.

A treasure basket

You could use this activity for a child observation.

1. Sit to one side and observe the child playing alone with the contents of the treasure chest. Write a detailed, timed observation of the activity, including the following points:

    - what the child does with each object
    - how long he or she plays with each object
    - what expressions or sounds he or she makes
    - how involved he or she is in the activity.

2. Evaluate the activity in terms of its value to the child's overall development and enjoyment.

3. What would you change if you were to repeat the activity?

▶ Puppet play

Make two simple finger puppets: one (large) for you, and the other (slightly smaller) for the child.

1. Using a square of felt, cut and stick or sew a small cap shape to fit over the finger. Decorate it with hair (wool) and a face.

2. Play a game in which the child copies your actions, such as:

    My little man bows down

    My little man turns round

    My little man jumps up and down

    And makes a funny sound – BOO!

This activity promotes manipulative skills, social and language development, and the development of imagination.

Chapter 9

Two years

B y 2 years, children can run, jump, kick, and use words as well as actions to express themselves.

They are curious and impulsive explorers of their environment, and want to be as independent as possible – starting to play independently.

Children easily become frustrated when they cannot express themselves or are prevented from doing something they want to do.

They may show strong emotions in 'temper tantrums' or bursting into tears – the classic 'terrible twos'. They are also affected by the emotions of others and will laugh or cry in sympathy.

Physical development

Gross motor skills

Children:
- can run safely, avoiding obstacles, and are very mobile
- can climb up onto furniture
- can throw a ball overhand, but cannot yet catch a ball
- push and pull large, wheeled toys
- walk up and down stairs, usually putting both feet on each step

Preparing to throw a ball overarm

- walk into a large ball when attempting to kick it
- sit on a tricycle and propel it with their feet – they cannot yet use the pedals
- squat with complete steadiness.

Riding a tricycle, propelling it with feet

Attempting to kick a large ball

By 2½ years, children:
- stand on tiptoe when shown how to do so
- climb nursery apparatus
- jump with both feet together from a low step
- kick a large ball, but gently and lopsidedly.

Fine motor skills

Children:
- draw circles, lines and dots using their preferred hand
- pick up tiny objects using a fine pincer grasp
- can build a tower of six or more blocks, with a longer concentration span
- enjoy picture books and turn the pages singly
- can copy a vertical line and sometimes a 'V' shape
- can drink from a cup with fewer spills, and manage scooping with a spoon at mealtimes.

Drinking confidently from a cup

By 2½ years, children:
- can hold a pencil in their preferred hand, with an improved tripod grasp
- can build a tower of seven or more cubes, using their preferred hand
- can imitate a horizontal line, a circle, a 'T' and a 'V'.

Sensory development

Children:
- recognise familiar people in photographs after being shown them once, but do not yet recognise themselves in photographs
- listen to general conversation with interest.

By 2½ years, children:
- recognise themselves in photos
- recognise minute details in picture books.

Cognitive and language development

Children:
- are particularly interested in the names of people and objects
- are beginning to understand the consequences of their own actions and those of others, for example when something falls over or breaks
- provide comfort when other babies cry – **empathy** requires a deep knowledge of other minds (younger babies cry when others cry)
- talk to themselves often, but may not always be understood by others
- now speak over 200 words, and accumulate new words very rapidly
- understand many more words than they can speak (possibly over a thousand)
- talk about an absent object when reminded of it – seeing an empty plate, for instance, they may say 'biscuit'
- often omit opening or closing consonants, so 'bus' may become 'us', or 'coat' become 'coa'
- use phrases as **telegraphic speech** (or **telegraphese**) – for example, 'daddy-car' might mean a number of different things, including 'Daddy's in his car', 'I want to go in Daddy's car' or 'Daddy's car is outside'
- spend a great deal of time in naming things and what they do, such as 'chair' or 'step' and 'up'
- follow simple instructions and requests, such as 'Please bring me the book'
- want to share songs, conversations and finger-rhymes more and more.

By 2½ years, children:
- know their full name
- still repeat words spoken to them (**echolalia**)
- continually ask questions beginning 'What … ?' or 'Who … ?'
- use the pronouns 'I', 'me' and 'you' correctly
- talk audibly and intelligibly to themselves when playing
- can say a few nursery rhymes.

Emotional and social development

Children:
- are beginning to express how they feel
- are impulsive and curious about their environment
- are eager to try out new experiences
- may be clingy and dependent at times, and self-reliant and independent at others
- often feel frustrated when unable to express themselves – about half of 2-year-old children have tantrums on a more or less daily basis
- can dress themselves independently
- often like to help others, but not when doing so conflicts with their own desires.

By 2½ years, children:
- eat skilfully with a spoon and may use a fork
- may be dry through the night (but there is wide variation)
- are emotionally still very dependent on an adult
- may go to the toilet independently; but may need sensitive help with pulling their pants up
- play more with other children, but may not share their toys with them.

Play

Children:
- love physical games, including running, jumping and climbing
- like to build with construction toys
- engage in more sustained role-play, such as putting dolls to bed or driving a car
- often play alone (**solitary play**) or watch other children playing (**spectator play**)

Spectator play

- may play alongside other children, but not with them (**parallel play**)

- enjoy playing **symbolically**, letting one thing stand for another (**pretend play**) – for example, children may pretend that they are tiny babies and crawl into a doll's bed, or push a block on the floor, pretending that it is a train: this rich **imaginative play** shows their minds at work and often reveals feelings that cannot be expressed in words

- enjoy helping around the house

- enjoy musical games.

Parallel play

Promoting development

- Provide toys to ride and climb on, and space to run and play.

- Encourage children to develop an interest in the natural world, including plants and wildlife.

- Encourage the use of safe climbing frames and sandpits, but always under supervision.

- Provide opportunities for messy play with water and paints.

- Encourage ball play (throwing and catching), to promote co-ordination skills.

- Provide bricks, sorting boxes, hammer-and-peg toys and simple jigsaw puzzles – these improve co-ordination and motor skills.

- Try offering triangular pencils to help improve pencil grasp.

- Rather than asking a child what they have drawn or painted – which may imply that only art that represents the real world is worthy of interest – ask them an open-ended question, such as 'Tell me all about your drawing'; show your interest in their work through praise and encouragement.

- Provide simple models to build (using materials such as Duplo®).

- Provide picture books, crayons and paper, and glove puppets.

- Be relaxed about toilet training – always praise children when they succeed, and do not show disapproval when they do not.

- Help children to learn how to express their feelings in ways that are honest and open but without hurting others.

- Provide play dough or soft clay. Encourage children to express their feelings – for instance, frustration can be expressed by pummelling and hitting the dough.

- Play simple games of 'Let's pretend'.

- Provide resources for role-play, including hats and clothes for dressing-up.

Activities

▶ Finger-painting

At first, painting is best done with the fingers as this frees children from having to control a brush and allows direct contact between the textures of the paint and the children themselves.

1   Protect the area and the child's clothes.

2   Place a large sheet of paper on the floor or a table – lining paper or the wrong side of wallpaper are cheap sources.

3   Arrange the prepared paint colours in a palette or on plates. Stand these on the paper also.

4   Encourage the child to use all the colours, and to mix them and see how the colours change.

Finger-paints may be bought ready-made, or you can make your own. Mix together:

- ½ cup of soap flakes – use real soap, not detergent

- ½ cup of cold water starch

- ¾ cup of cold water

- food colourings.

This activity promotes the development of manipulative skills and sensory, cognitive and language development.

▶ Modelling with play dough

Modelling or just manipulating play dough enables children to learn about different materials, gives scope to their imagination, and is a soothing and relaxing activity.

Try the play-dough recipe below – this dough lasts well when stored in a plastic bag or box in the fridge, and it has a good texture for young children to handle.

Play-dough recipe:

- 1 cup of water
- 1 tablespoon of cooking oil
- 1 heaped cup of plain flour
- 1 cup of salt
- 2 teaspoons of cream of tartar
- food colouring as required.

To make the play dough:

1 Mix the water, the oil and a few drops of food colouring in a pan. Heat gently.

2 Add the rest of the ingredients and stir.

3 The dough will start to form and will lift away from the pan. Turn off the heat. Remove the dough from the pan and leave it to cool.

Allow the child to handle the dough freely at first to explore the possibilities. Then you could provide a variety of tools for play cooking, for example shape cutters, a rolling pin, plastic knives, a spatula, and some small plastic bowls and plates.

SafetyPoints

When making the dough you can let children help with the measuring, but take extreme care to keep the hot saucepan away from their reach.

Dough made according to the recipe above will last for up to a month if kept wrapped in the fridge. If using other recipes, follow the instructions for storage and use.

Make sure that children do not *eat* the dough – even commercially made play dough includes ordinary flour (about 40 per cent of the mixture). Extra vigilance is needed by staff to stop children with **coeliac disease** putting the dough into their mouth.

Chapter 10

Three years

Children now demonstrate that they have an inner world of thought and that they can talk about this.

Their drawings and paintings are beginning to include recognisable representations of people and things.

They now play with other children rather than just near them, and are making their first friends.

Physical development

Gross motor skills

Children:
- can jump from a low step
- can walk backwards and sideways
- can stand and walk on tiptoe, and stand on one foot
- can ride a tricycle using pedals

Catching a ball

Riding a tricycle using the pedals

Kicking a ball with force

- climb stairs with one foot on each step, and go downwards with two feet on each step
- have good spatial awareness – they can manoeuvre themselves around objects
- can throw a ball overhand, and can catch a large ball with arms outstretched

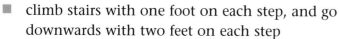

- use their whole body to kick a ball with force.

Fine motor skills

Children:
- can copy a building pattern of three or more cubes, including a bridge
- can build towers of nine or ten cubes

Copying a building pattern, including a bridge

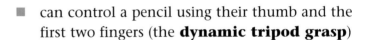

- can control a pencil using their thumb and the first two fingers (the **dynamic tripod grasp**)
- can copy a circle and the letters 'V', 'H' and 'T'
- enjoy standing at an easel and painting with a large brush

Building a tower of cubes

Drawing a face

- can draw a person with a head, and sometimes with legs and (later) arms coming out from the head – squiggles inside the head represent a face
- can cut paper with scissors
- can thread large beads onto a lace
- can eat using a fork or spoon.

In China children of 3 years of age are able to eat with chopsticks, whereas the competent use of knives and forks in other cultures usually starts at age 5. It is thought that this cultural difference is due to early encouragement and a great deal of practice rather than to a greater inborn manual dexterity.

Copying a circle, using a dynamic tripod grasp

Cognitive and language development

Children:
- can match two or three primary colours, usually red and yellow, but sometimes confuse blue and green colours
- begin to understand the concept of time – they remember events in the past and can anticipate events in the future
- are fascinated by cause and effect, and often ask 'Why?'
- can sort objects into simple categories
- remember and repeat songs and nursery rhymes
- understand the concept of 'one' and 'lots'
- count by rote up to ten, but do not appreciate quantity beyond two or three
- use personal pronouns and plurals correctly and can give their own name and sex, and sometimes age
- carry on simple conversations, often missing link words such as 'the' and 'is'
- learn to speak more than one language if they hear more than one language spoken around them as they grow
- still talk to themselves when playing
- enjoy listening to and making music
- can control their attention, choosing to stop an activity and return to it without much difficulty.

Emotional and social development

Children:
- like to do things unaided
- enjoy family mealtimes
- can think about things from someone else's point of view
- show affection for younger siblings
- manage to use the lavatory independently, and are often dry through the night (though this is variable between children, and from day to day with a given child)
- enjoy helping adults, as in tidying up
- are willing to share toys with other children and are beginning to take turns when playing
- often develop fears, for example of the dark, as they become capable of pretending and imagining
- are becoming aware of being male or female (are developing a gender role)
- make friends and are interested in having friends.

Moral and spiritual development

Children:
- are beginning to develop the concept of being helpful
- believe that all rules are fixed and unchallengeable – for example, if told that coats must be worn when playing outside, they accept this without question.

Play

Children:
- like to ride tricycles and play outdoors
- enjoy simple craft activities, for example with scissors and beads, and playing with dough
- join in active pretend play with other children
- enjoy playing on the floor with bricks, boxes, trains and dolls, both alone and with others
- like jigsaw puzzles and making models.

Playing with other children

Promoting development

- Provide a wide variety of playthings – balls for throwing and catching, sand, jigsaw puzzles and so on.

- Encourage play with other children.

- Provide a variety of art and craft activities: thick crayons, stubby paintbrushes, paper, paint, and dough for modelling or play cooking.

- Talk to children often and read to them, to encourage the development of language.

- Encourage children to use their fingers to help count to ten. They will begin to learn that five and five make ten, and they can fold down four fingers and see that there are six fingers still up.

- Encourage swimming and trips to the park. Children may even enjoy longer walks.

- Promote independence by teaching children how to look after and put away their own clothes and toys.

- Provide toys for water play, perhaps in the bath or paddling pool.

- Let them help you cook – you could make some biscuits.

- Encourage visits to the library and story times.

- Play simple matching and sorting games with them, such as lotto.

Watching TV, videos, DVDs

Limit the amount of TV children watch; 10–15 minute periods are about right for this age group.

Be selective: prepare children for a programme or video that is due to start and switch the TV off after the programme has finished.

Choose programmes that are fairly slow-paced and which emphasise interactivity; ones which inspire children to make sounds or to sing and dance are good.

Avoid busy cartoon adventures, which can be very noisy.

Watch TV with children where possible, so that you are there to explain what is happening and to encourage questions.

Extend the programme's content with activities or books; for example, if a programme such as Teletubbies explores the concept of number, follow through with a counting song.

Using computers

Computer use for most children under age 3 does not have meaning for the child. See ICT Guidelines for children aged 3 to 5 years on page 93.

See ICT Guidelines for children aged 3 to 5 years on page 93.

Safety *Points*

During cookery activities, never let the child use the oven or handle hot liquids. Make sure that any spills are wiped up promptly.

If cooking within a nursery setting, keep the maximum number of children to four.

Always supervise water play.

Activities

▶ Making music using instruments

You can help children to make a range of percussive (beating) and shaking instruments.

1   Collect together tins to beat with wooden spoons, saucepan lids to clash together, and securely closed jars containing pasta or pulses to shake.

2   Look for anything that children can safely manipulate and that makes an interesting sound.

Making music together

The voice is the most natural musical instrument there is. As well as speaking and singing with it, you can make a whole range of different sounds. This activity encourages experimentation and, with the help of a tape recorder, allows children to find out what they can do with their voice.

1   You need a portable tape recorder with a built-in microphone.

2   If the child is not already familiar with it, demonstrate the workings of the tape recorder.

3   You could start off with the child singing a favourite song or rhyme, then play the tape back to hear how it sounds. You could talk about the different sounds on the tape, and begin to describe them.

4   Try the following ideas:

  ▪ Speak in a very high and very low voice.

  ▪ Speak very fast or very slowly.

  ▪ Whisper very quietly – close to the microphone.

  ▪ Shout – a long way from the microphone!

  ▪ Make animal noises.

  ▪ Hum a tune.

1   Make a detailed observation of the activity.

2   Outline the possible benefits to the child, and write an evaluation.

▶ Picture lotto

You can buy a ready-made lotto game, but you might enjoy making your own.

1   Find some suitable illustrations for a simple picture lotto game.

2   Make your picture lotto game by pasting three sets of eight or more coloured pictures of toys or household objects onto three large pieces of card. Cut round the pictures on two of the cards, leaving one as your playing board.

3   To play lotto, simply fill up the playing board by turning over cards that match.

Games such as lotto encourage the concept of one-to-one correspondence, which is vital for the child's understanding of number.

Playing picture lotto

If you have access to the Internet, you could collect some interesting pictures by visiting the BBC Education website, for example, to print pictures of the Tweenies or other characters.

Chapter 11

Four years

At 4 years of age, children are quite capable and independent.

They walk with swinging steps, almost like an adult's, and like to hop and jump.

Children are fascinated by cause and effect, and their increasing mastery of language prompts them to ask questions about the way things work in the world.

Physical development

Gross motor skills

Children: ■ have developed a good sense of
balance and may be able to walk
along a line

Moving with a good
sense of balance

Running on tiptoe

■ can stand, walk and run on tiptoe

■ can catch, kick, throw and bounce a ball

■ bend at the waist to pick up objects from
the floor

■ enjoy climbing trees and on frames

■ run up and down stairs, one foot per step

■ can ride a tricycle with skill and make sharp
turns easily.

Bouncing a ball

Fine motor skills

Children:
- can build a tower of ten or more cubes
- can copy a building pattern of three steps using six cubes or more

Copying a building pattern with more than six bricks

- are able to thread small beads on a lace
- hold and use a pencil or pen in an adult fashion
- can draw on request a figure that resembles a person, showing head, legs and body
- can copy the letters 'X', 'V', 'H', 'T' and 'O'
- can spread their hand, and can bring their thumbs into opposition with each finger in turn.

Holding a pen in an adult fashion

Sensory development

Children: ■ match and name primary colours

■ listen to long stories with attention.

Sharing a picture book

Cognitive and language development

Children: ■ enjoy counting up to 20 by rote, and understand the concept of number up to three

■ talk about things in the past and the future

■ can sort objects into groups

■ have increased memory skills – for example, they can remember a particular event, such as when their grandparents visited several months previously

■ can give reasons and solve problems

■ include more detail in their drawings, such as adding hands and fingers to drawings of people

■ often confuse fact with fiction

■ talk fluently, asking questions ('Why … ?', 'When … ?', 'How … ?') and understanding the answers

■ can repeat nursery rhymes and songs, with very few errors

■ can state their full name and address almost correctly

■ tell long stories, sometimes confusing fact and fantasy

■ enjoy jokes and plays on words

■ may begin to recognise patterns in the way words are formed and apply these consistently, unaware that many common words have irregular forms – for example, as the past tense is often made by adding '-ed' ('I walk' becomes 'I walked'), children may say 'I runned' or 'I goed' instead of 'I ran' or 'I went'.

Emotional and social development

Children:
- can eat skilfully with a spoon and a fork
- can wash and dry their hands, and brush their teeth
- can undress and dress themselves, except for laces, ties and back buttons
- often show sensitivity to others
- show a sense of humour, both in talk and in activities
- like to be independent and are strongly self-willed
- like to be with other children.

Dressing unaided

Moral and spiritual development

Children:
- understand the needs of others and the need to share and take turns
- try to work out what is 'right' and what is 'wrong' in behaviour.

Play

Children:
- act out puppet shows and scenes they have seen on television
- play elaborate role-play games with others
- enjoy imaginative play, which helps them to cope with strong emotions.

Promoting development

- Provide children with plenty of opportunities for exercise.
- Play party games such as musical statues to foster the ideas of winning, losing and co-operation.
- Encourage children to use rope swings and climbing frames.
- Encourage play with small construction toys, jigsaw puzzles and board games.
- Provide art and craft materials for painting, printing, and gluing and sticking activities.
- Encourage sand and water play, and play with dough or modelling clay.
- Talk often with children. Repeat favourite stories and encourage them to express themselves.
- Visit the library and read books together.
- Look for books and puzzles that help children to categorise and sort objects.
- Play lotto and other matching games such as pairs (pelmanism).
- Display children's paintings around the house – this gives them a feeling of pride in their work.
- Teach children how to dress and undress themselves in preparation for school games lessons.
- Encourage independence when going to the toilet.
- Let children practise using a computer mouse and carrying out simple computer activities.

- Organise visits to parks and farms. Encourage children to draw what they have seen.

- Involve children in caring for pets to encourage a sense of responsibility.

- Provide a box of dressing-up clothes for imaginative play.

- Let children organise their own games with friends, to encourage independence and confidence.

- Try not to rush to help when children are finding an activity difficult – allow them time to master new skills, offering praise and encouragement.

Activities

▶ Making a book

Helping children to make a book of their own is a good way of encouraging a liking for books.

One idea is to make a book about the child and about the people and things that mean a lot to her or him. This could include drawings or photographs of:

- family and friends

- toys and favourite things

- birthdays and holidays

- pets and other animals

- favourite foods and games.

The book need not be elaborate; the main idea is to involve the child in the making of it and thereby increase her or his **self-esteem**. You could buy a scrapbook or a large notebook, or just fold some large sheets of paper in half, punch holes along the fold, and thread some ribbon or cord through them.

Growing mustard and cress

Children will enjoy growing their own plants and discovering how to care for them.

1   Collect some empty eggshells. Give each child a shell and ask them to draw a face on their own shell.

2   Cut a cardboard egg carton into individual pockets. Place one eggshell in each pocket.

3   Pack each shell generously with cotton wool and soak this with water before putting the seeds on top.

4   Water the cotton wool regularly and wait for the 'green hair' to sprout. (This should only take two or three days.)

Five years

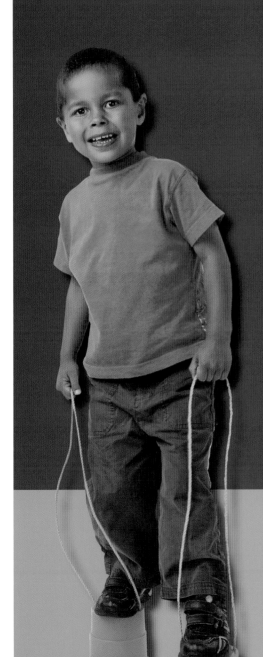

Children enjoy showing what they can do – hopping, skipping, dancing and playing group ball games.

They have a growing awareness of the world, and their language shows this understanding.

Children are learning self-control, including how to wait and how to take turns.

They are completely independent in everyday skills, such as washing, dressing and eating.

Physical development

Gross motor skills

Children:

- have increased agility – they can run and dodge, run lightly on their toes, climb and skip

- show good balance – they can stand on one foot for about ten seconds, and some may ride a bike without stabilisers

- show good co-ordination, playing ball games and dancing rhythmically to music

- can bend at the waist and touch their toes without bending at the knees

- can hop 2–3 m (6–9 feet) forwards on each foot separately

- use a variety of play equipment, including slides, swings and climbing frames.

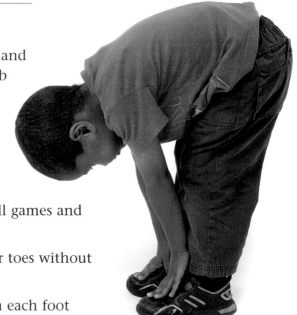

Bending at the waist and touching the toes

Fine motor skills

Children:

- can use a knife and fork competently, but may still need to have meat cut up for them

- may be able to thread a large-eyed needle and sew with large stitches

- have good control over pencils and paint brushes

- can draw a person with a head, a body, arms, legs, a nose, a mouth and eyes

- can copy elaborate models, such as a four-step model using ten cubes

Drawing a person

- can construct elaborate models using kits (such as Duplo®)
- can copy a square and, at 5½ years, a triangle
- can copy letters 'V', 'T', 'H', 'O', 'X', 'L', 'A', 'C', 'U' and 'Y'
- can count the fingers on one hand using the index finger of the other
- can do jigsaw puzzles with interlocking pieces.

Constructing an elaborate model

Sensory development

Children: ■ can match ten or twelve colours.

Cognitive and language development

Children: ■ produce drawings with good detail – for example, a house with windows, a door, a roof and a chimney

■ ask about abstract words (for instance, 'What does "beyond" mean?')

■ can give their full name, age and address, and often their birthday

■ are interested in reading and writing

■ recognise their name and attempt to write it

■ talk about the past, present and future, with a good sense of time

■ are fluent in their speech and grammatically correct for the most part

■ love to be read stories and will then act them out in detail later, either alone or with friends

■ enjoy jokes and riddles.

Emotional and social development

Children:
- dress and undress alone, but may have difficulty with shoelaces
- have very definite likes and dislikes, some with little apparent logic – for example, a child might eat carrots when cut into strips but not when cut into rounds
- are able to amuse themselves for longer periods of time, for example looking at a book or watching a video
- show sympathy and comfort friends who are hurt
- enjoy caring for pets
- choose their own friends.

Moral and spiritual development

Children:
- understand the social rules of their culture, for example the usual way to greet somebody
- instinctively help other children when they are distressed.

Play

Children:
- enjoy team games and games with rules
- may show a preference for a particular sport or craft activity
- play complicated games on the floor with miniature objects (**small-world play**)
- play alone or with others, including younger children
- enjoy elaborate pretend play with others.

Playing with a younger child

Using computers

Computers should supplement – and not replace – activities such as art, sand and water play, music, outdoor exploration, reading stories together or sharing conversations and socialising with other children. Using the computer should be just one of many activity choices for children to explore. For computer activities to be successful with young children, adults should:

- observe the way children use the computer to solve problems

- monitor the amount of time spent at the computer

- avoid telling children what to do next, but be available to help them work out what to do for themselves

- encourage children to work with another child to promote the social skills of turn-taking and sharing

- talk with them about their activities and be on hand to answer questions

- extend and reinforce the learning: this means applying the lessons learned at the computer to other activities, such as games, identifying numbers, shapes or letters, or acting out stories from the program.

The software selected must be developmentally appropriate – that is, consistent with how children develop and learn – and should also fit their need to interact with their environment. Software for young children should:

- encourage exploration, imagination and problem-solving

- reflect and build on what children already know

- involve many senses and include sound, music and voice

- be open-ended: it should encourage creativity, language skills, early reading skills and problem-solving, with the child in control of the pace and the direction

- provide equal opportunities for all children; for example, software should be easily adaptable to children who have a hearing or sight problem.

Chapter **12** Five years

Promoting development

- Provide plenty of outdoor activities.

- Provide stilts to encourage balance and co-ordination – these could be made from old paint cans and strong cord.

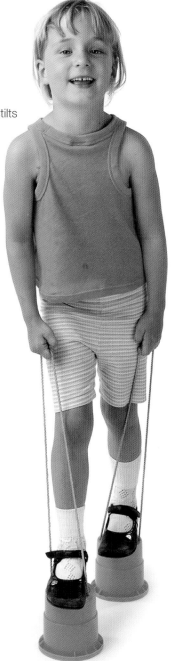

Balancing on stilts

- Teach children to ride a two-wheeled bicycle.

- Teach children to swim.

- Encourage non-stereotypical activities, such as boys using skipping ropes and girls playing football.

- Team sports may be provided at school or at clubs such as Beavers, Rainbows and Woodcraft Folk.

- Encourage the use of models, jigsaws, sewing kits and craft activities, as well as drawing and painting.

- Talk to children about past, present and future, to promote language skills.

- Allow children to organise their own games.

- Encourage children to help with simple tasks, such as washing-up or watering plants.

- Set clear boundaries for behaviour, and always explain these to children.

SafetyPoints

If you have large picture windows, mark them with coloured strips to make it obvious when they are closed.

When out at dusk or when walking on country roads without pavements, use luminous armbands or light-coloured clothing for children.

Activities

▷ Conservation of number

Conservation is the name for the concept that objects remain the same in fundamental ways, such as in their volume or number, even when there are external changes in their shape or arrangement.

This activity uses plastic teddy bears but you could also use buttons. The object of the activity is to see whether the child recognises that the same number of bears remain, even when they have been arranged differently.

1 Make two rows of objects. Check that the child agrees that the two rows contain the same number in each row.

2 Spread one row out to make a longer row. Ask the child which row contains *more* objects.

Checking that the number of objects in each row is the same

Ideas for students

Jean Piaget (1896–1980) was a psychologist who studied the way in which children develop intellectually. Piaget stated that children under 7 years old would not **conserve** when presented with the activity above. However, other researchers have found that children as young as 5 or 6 years old are able to understand that objects remain the same, even when arranged differently.

1 You could try this simple experiment with several children aged 5, 6 and 7 years old.

2 Summarise your findings.

Feeding the birds

This activity encourages the development of caring for living things, knowledge and understanding of the natural world, and manual dexterity. It is particularly suitable for a winter's day.

First you could talk to the child about the birds in wintertime:

- Why will it be difficult for them to find food?

- How could you help them?

Then you could suggest that you make the birds some bird 'cakes'. You will need:

- mixed garden bird food (or you can mix your own from finely chopped nuts, millet, oatmeal, sunflower seed, chopped apple and dried fruit)

- empty yogurt pots

- lengths of string

- lard or suet

- a mixing bowl

- a tray and a wooden spoon.

Making the bird cakes:

1 Encourage the child to mix all the dry ingredients in the bowl, using the wooden spoon.

2 In the meantime, start to melt the lard or suet very carefully, well out of the child's reach.

3 Make a large, chunky knot at one end of a piece of string. Coil that end at the base of the yoghurt pot, leaving a good tail coming out at the top of the pot.

4 Help the child to spoon the dry mixture into the pots all around the string. Leave about 2 cm (1 inch) at the top still to fill.

5 Place your filled pots on a tray and lift this out of the child's reach.

6 Carefully pour the melted fat around the mixture. Stir it in, and put the 'cakes' in a cool, safe place to set.

7 When set, remove the bird cake from the pots. Go with the child to tie them up. Hang them where you will have a good view from a window, and make sure that they are well out of the reach of cats.

Remember that when you start to feed birds, they come to depend on you as a food source. Having started, you need to continue to feed them throughout the winter.

You could use a bird book to identify your visitors, and a bird diary to remember their names.

Six years

Children of 6 years are full of curiosity, and are developing their own interests.

They are forming new concepts of size, shape, weight and distance.

They are growing towards reading and writing independently, putting words and ideas down on paper, and often using invented spelling.

Physical development

Children:
- are gaining in both strength and agility; they can jump off apparatus at school with confidence

- can run and jump, and can kick a football up to 6 m (18 feet)

Jumping with confidence

Jumping off apparatus

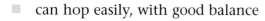

- can hop easily, with good balance

- can catch and throw balls with accuracy

- can ride a two-wheeled bike, possibly without stabilisers

- can skip in time to music, alternating their feet.

Hopping with good balance

Children:
- can build a tower of cubes that is virtually straight
- can hold a pen or pencil in a way similar to that of an adult (the **dynamic tripod grasp**)
- are able to write a number of letters of similar size
- can write their last name as well as their first name
- may begin to write simple stories.

Building straight towers

Using a pen with a dynamic tripod grasp

Writing a name

Cognitive and language development

Children:
- begin to think in a more co-ordinated way, and can hold more than one point of view at a time
- begin to develop concepts of quantity: length, measurement, distance, area, time, volume, capacity and weight
- are able to distinguish the difference between reality and fantasy, but are often still frightened by supernatural characters in books, on the television and so on

Exploring concepts of quantity

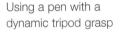

Chapter 13 Six years

- are interested in basic scientific principles and are beginning to understand, for example, what happens to everyday materials if they are soaked or heated
- are increasingly influenced by cultural conventions in drawing and writing, for example often combining their own personal symbols with letters from the alphabet
- draw people in detail including, for instance, eyebrows and eyelashes, and buttons and laces on clothes
- can pronounce the majority of the sounds of their own language
- talk fluently and with confidence
- can remember and repeat nursery rhymes and songs
- are steadily developing **literacy** skills (reading and writing), although the ability to read independently with confidence usually begins between 7 and 9 years of age
- alternate between wanting stories read to them and reading books themselves.

Emotional and social development

Children:
- can carry out simple tasks, such as peeling vegetables, watering plants, hanging up clothes and tidying the contents of drawers
- choose friends mainly because of their personality and interests
- can hold a long conversation with another child or an adult, naturally taking turns in speaking and listening
- begin to compare themselves with other people – 'I am like her in that way, but different in this way...'

Moral and spiritual development

Children:
- are beginning to develop further concepts, such as forgiveness and fairness.

Play

Children:
- play together with other children (**co-operative play**)
- assign roles to others in elaborate pretend play and role-play
- role-play situations of which they have no direct experience but which might happen to them one day, such as getting married or travelling through space to the moon (**fantasy play**).

Promoting development

- Provide opportunity for vigorous exercise.
- Allow children to try a new activity or sport, such as football, dancing, judo or gymnastics.
- Encourage writing skills by providing lots of examples of things written for different purposes, such as shopping lists, letters and recipes.
- Play memory games with children, such as pairs and dominoes.
- Talk to children about what they have done during the day.
- Encourage children to sort and match objects. Ask them to order things according to more abstract concepts, such as sweetness or preference.
- Try not to correct grammatical mistakes – instead, respond by subtly rephrasing their statement while showing that you have understood them. Thus a child might say, 'A lion is more fiercer than a cat', and you could reply, 'Yes, lions are fiercer than cats'.
- Create a warm, supporting atmosphere during story time at home or at school, with plenty of talk about the story you are reading.

SafetyPoints

Give children clear guidelines about safety. For example:

- never climb a tree without first asking an adult's permission
- never cross a road without an accompanying adult
- never accept anything offered by a stranger
- never, ever go anywhere with a stranger.

Activities

▶ Cooking biscuits

Making biscuits gives plenty of opportunities for measuring, mixing, rolling out, cutting shapes and decorating.

Get together everything you will need before you begin, so that you do not have to leave children unsupervised. If cooking at school, limit the number of children to four. Follow these guidelines:

- Teach children to wash their hands and dry them thoroughly before cooking.

- Teach them to be very careful when handling knives.

- Teach them to ask before tasting anything.

- Clear up any spills immediately.

Making biscuits

Here is a basic biscuit recipe:

- 125 g (4 oz) soft margarine or butter
- 125 g (4 oz) sugar (white or brown)
- 250 g (8 oz) plain flour
- 1 egg
- pinch of salt
- grated orange or lemon rind if desired.

Making the biscuits:

1 Pre-heat the oven (moderate: 190°C, 375°F or gas mark 5).

2 Beat the margarine and sugar together.

3 Beat the egg and add to the mixture.

4 Sift in the flour and the salt (and the grated rind, if used).

5 Mix to form a ball of dough.

6 Roll out the dough to a thickness of 0.5 cm (¼ inch). Cut into shapes.

7 Put the shapes on a greased baking tray, and bake them in the middle of the oven for about 15 minutes.

Make a detailed observation of the activity. Notice the language used by the children and the understanding of concepts that they demonstrate.

▶ Early science

Try out this simple demonstration of static electricity with a child or a group of children.

1 Stir a little salt and pepper together.

2 Ask the child to separate them using a teaspoon. This, of course, is not possible.

3 Then rub the spoon against a sweater – ideally one made of acrylic or another synthetic fibre. This creates static electricity on the spoon.

4 Simply hold the spoon just above the mixture. Pepper is lighter than salt, and the static electricity on the spoon will lift it free.

Chapter 14

Seven years

Children at 7 have a well-developed sense of balance and enjoy activities that involve precise movements, such as hopscotch or skipping games.

They are interested in talking, listening, and reading and writing, and enjoy games with rules.

They have a clear sense of right and wrong, and see friendships as very important.

Physical development

Gross motor skills

Children:
- can hop on either leg, and can walk along a thin line with their arms outstretched for balance

- may be expert at riding a two-wheeled bike or using roller skates

- can climb on play apparatus with skill, some managing to climb ropes

- have increased stamina, shown in activities such as swimming, skating, gymnastics and martial arts

- are able to control their speed when running and can swerve to avoid collision

- are skilful in catching and throwing a ball, using one hand only.

Walking along a narrow pole

Catching a ball with one hand

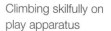

Climbing skilfully on play apparatus

Fine motor skills

Children:
- can build tall, straight towers with cubes
- are more competent in their writing skills – individual letters are more clearly differentiated now, and capital and small letters are in proportion
- begin to use colour in a naturalistic way, for example using a band of green colour at the bottom of the page to represent grass, and a band of blue across the top to represent sky
- draw people with heads, bodies, hands, hair, fingers and clothes
- can use a large needle to sew with thread.

Drawing a person in detail

Cognitive and language development

Children:
- are able to **conserve** number – for example, they know that there are ten sweets whether they are pushed close together or spread apart
- express themselves in speech and writing
- can use a computer mouse and keyboard for simple word processing
- enjoy the challenge of experimenting with new materials, and enjoy learning mathematical and scientific concepts, such as adding and subtracting numbers
- perform simple calculations in their head
- begin to understand how to tell the time

Enjoying learning about living things

- may be interested in design and in working models
- enjoy learning about living things and about the world around them
- are able to arrive at logical conclusions and to understand cause and effect.

Emotional and social development

Children:
- learn how to control their emotions – they realise that they can keep their own thoughts private and hide their true feelings
- begin to think in terms not only of who they are, but also of who they would like to be
- are completely independent in washing, dressing and toileting skills
- may be able to speak up for themselves, for example when visiting the dentist or the doctor
- may be critical of their own work at school
- form close friendships, mostly within their own sex.

Moral and spiritual development

Children:
- have a clear sense of right and wrong – for example, they realise that it is wrong to hurt other people physically
- express feelings of awe and wonder, particularly about nature, plants and insects.

Play

Children:
- engage in complex co-operative play, using more people, props and ideas
- take part in games with rules.

Using computers

As children increasingly develop language and literacy skills, they are no longer limited to icons and pictures on the screen for understanding. Simple word processors become important educational tools as children experiment with written language. By now, the teacher still needs to monitor what children do, but they are increasingly able to choose and direct their own activities.

Using tape recorders

Using tape recorders promotes early literacy skills: speaking listening, reading and writing. Apart from following the text in a book while listening to a taped story, children can also record their own made-up stories, poems and songs, or record themselves reading aloud. Adults can then transcribe their stories – or write them down – using the children's own recorded words. In this way, children can see how the spoken word can turn into the written word.

Cameras

Cameras – both still and video – can provide a useful record of children's activities while they are at work, as well as performances and special events. These photos or films can then be added to, with children writing a storyboard or simply providing captions to the photos.

Promoting development

- Encourage vigorous outdoor play – on swings and climbing frames, and in skipping and hopping games such as hopscotch.

- Take children swimming, skating or riding, or to a dancing or martial arts class.

- Arrange an obstacle course for children to navigate bikes around.

- Provide a range of drawing and craft materials, such as charcoal, paint, clay and materials for collage.

- Help children to make a safe 'den', using a tepee design with sticks and a blanket.

- Encourage children in simple gardening skills, such as digging, planting, raking and watering.

- Promote creative expression in the form of written stories, poetry, dance, drama and making music.

- Take children to see plays and puppet shows.

- Involve children in a puppet show – both in making the puppets and in acting out a play.

- Try some simple cause-and-effect experiments. For example, you could demonstrate how a waterwheel works.

- Try growing some simple crystals.

- Encourage children to plan and make working models, such as cranes, pulley lifts and wheeled vehicles, using recycled materials.

- Introduce children to the customs of different religions, such as Diwali, Ramadan and Christmas.

- Encourage children to become more familiar with using a computer, for instance keying in letters, numbers and punctuation marks.

- Encourage children to share stories together – even a child who is not yet fluent at reading will still enjoy trying to read to a younger child.

- Allow children to run simple errands on their own, for example to post a letter.

SafetyPoints

Teach children never to put a plastic bag on their head.

Teach children only ever to buy sweets from a shop and never to accept them from a stranger.

Activities

▶ Number bonds

This is a game that can be played by two people. One player calls out a number under ten. The other player answers with the number that brings the total of the two numbers to ten.

This has to be done as quickly as possible: if you hesitate, you are out! For example:

Player 1, 'Six'; Player 2, 'Four'.

Player 1, 'Two'; Player 2, 'Eight'.

Player 1, 'Three'; Player 2, 'Er… er…!'

Player 2 is out! Take it in turns to go first. Before you start, decide how many times you are going to play the game.

When the child is confident about numbers adding up to ten, you can vary the game by moving up to a larger number. Try twenty. Then go on to one hundred. Children will need a little more time to think as the numbers get bigger.

▶ A sound experiment

Make a yogurt-pot telephone.

You will need:

- two empty, clean yogurt pots
- a ball of string
- scissors.

To make the telephone:

1 Using the scissors, make a small hole in the bottom of each of the pots.

2 Cut a very long piece of string, and push one end through the bottom of each pot.

3 Tie a knot inside each pot to stop the string from coming out.

4 Ask a child to hold one of the pots to his or her ear. Now move away from the child until the string is straight and pulled tight. (You could do this yourself, or give the second pot to another child.)

5 Now send a telephone message to the child by speaking into the pot.

Children will learn that the sound of a voice makes the pot vibrate, and that the vibrations pass as sound waves along the string to the other pot and into the other person's ear.

°Nutrition Guidelines

Healthy eating plan for young children

Healthy, growing children need lots of energy, which must be supplied by the diet. Children should be encouraged to be as active as possible, and their diet must supply energy through frequent meals and snacks based on the main food groups, with limited fatty and sugary snacks.

Continued overleaf

Food groups	Main nutrients	Types to choose	Portions per day	Suggestions for meals and snacks
1 Bread, other cereals and potatoes All types of bread, rice, breakfast cereals, pasta, noodles and potatoes (beans and lentils can be eaten as part of this group)	Carbohydrate (starch), fibre, some calcium and iron, B-group vitamins	Wholemeal, brown, wholegrain or high-fibre versions of bread; avoid fried foods too often – e.g. chips. Use butter and other spreads sparingly	FIVE All meals of the day should include foods from this group As a proportion of the total meal, these foods should make up about one-third of the plate	One portion = • 1 bowl of breakfast cereal • 2 tablespoons (tbs) pasta or rice • 1 small potato Snack meals include bread or pizza
2 Fruit and vegetables Fresh, frozen and canned fruit and vegetables, dried fruit, fruit juice (beans and lentils can be eaten as part of this group)	Vitamin C, carotenes, iron, calcium, folate, fibre and some carbohydrate	Eat a wide variety of fruit and vegetables; avoid adding rich sauces to vegetables and sugar to fruit	FOUR/FIVE Daily; include 1 fruit or vegetable high in vitamin C, e.g. tomato, sweet pepper, orange or kiwi fruit	One portion = • 1 glass of pure fruit juice • 1 piece of fruit • 1 sliced tomato • 2 tbs cooked vegetables • 1 tbs of dried fruit – e.g. raisins
3 Milk and dairy foods Milk, cheese, yogurt and fromage frais (This group does not contain butter, eggs and cream)	Calcium, protein, B-group vitamins (particularly B12), vitamins A and D	Milk is a very good source of calcium, but calcium can also be obtained from cheese, flavoured or plain yogurts and fromage frais	THREE Children require the equivalent of one pint (500 ml) of milk each day to ensure an adequate amount of calcium For children under 2 years: use full-fat milk, yogurt and fromage frais. Over 2 years: can change to semi-skimmed milk, which provides less energy	One portion = • 1 glass of milk: (125 ml for a 1–3 year-old; 150–250 ml for older children) • 1 pot of yogurt or fromage frais • 1 tbs grated cheese (e.g. on pizza)
4 Meat, fish and alternatives Lean meat, poultry, fish, tofu, quorn, pulses (peas, beans, lentils), nuts and seeds	Iron, protein, B-group vitamins (particularly B12), zinc and magnesium	Lower-fat versions of meat with fat cut off, chicken without skin, etc. Beans and lentils are good alternatives, being low in fat and high in fibre	ONE/TWO Vegetarian children need 2–3 portions each day, because iron from vegetarian sources is not as easily absorbed as that from meat and fish; also give a good source of vitamin C to boost iron absorption	One portion = • 2 fish fingers (for a 3-year-old) • 4 fish fingers (for a 7-year-old) • baked beans • a small piece of chicken.
5 Fatty and sugary foods Margarine, low-fat spread, butter, ghee, cream, chocolate, crisps, biscuits, sweets and sugar,	Vitamins and essential fatty acids, but also a lot of fat, sugar and salt	Only offer small amounts of sugary and fatty foods. Fats and oils are found in all the other food groups	NONE Only eat fatty and sugary foods sparingly	Children may be offered foods with extra fat or sugar – biscuits, crisps, cakes and chocolate – as long as they are not replacing food from the other more nutritious main food groups

Chapter 15

Eight to twelve years

B etween the ages of 8 and 12, there may be quite a marked difference in the size and abilities of children. Most girls experience the start of **puberty** between the ages of 9 and 13; boys first experience puberty between the ages of 10 and 16. The timing of the onset of puberty will affect the way children get along with others, how they feel about themselves and what they do. Friends become increasingly important, as do having the right clothes and the right look.

Physical development

Children's height and weight continue to grow at a steady rate, and both strength and physical co-ordination skills are also increasing. Typically, children are very energetic and have a large appetite.

Gross motor skills

Children aged 8 and 9 years:

- have increased body strength and co-ordination and a quicker reaction time
- can ride a two-wheel bicycle easily
- can skip freely
- enjoy active, energetic games and sports
- often enjoy participating in competitive sports.

Children aged 10 and 11 years:

- differ in physical maturity; because girls experience **puberty** earlier they are generally as much as two years ahead of boys
- have body proportions that are becoming similar to those of adults.

Fine motor skills

Children aged 8 and 9 years:

- have more control over small muscles, and therefore write and draw with greater skill and dexterity
- draw people with details of clothing and facial features
- draw in a more naturalistic way; ways of showing depth, shading, three-dimensions and movement begin to develop
- are beginning to join letters together in handwriting.

Writing with joined-up handwriting

- tackle more detailed tasks such as needlework or woodwork

- have an established writing style, usually with joined-up letters.

Cognitive and language development

Children aged 8 and 9 years:

- have an increased ability to remember and pay attention, and to speak and express their ideas

- are learning to plan ahead and evaluate what they do

- have an increased ability to think and to reason

- can deal with abstract ideas

- use and understand complex sentences

- are highly verbal and enjoy making up and telling jokes

- can read stories with increasing fluency

- enjoy different types of activities – such as joining clubs, playing games with rules and collecting things

- enjoy projects that are task-oriented, such as sewing and woodwork

- use reference books with increasing skill.

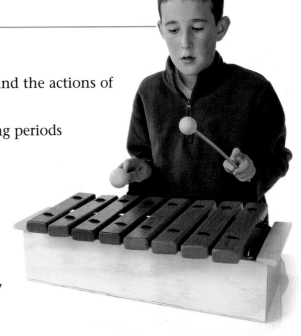

Children aged 10 and 11 years:

- begin to understand the motives behind the actions of another

- can concentrate on tasks for increasing periods

- can write fairly lengthy essays

- begin to devise memory strategies

- may be curious about drugs, alcohol and tobacco

- may develop special talents, showing particular skills in writing, maths, art, music or woodwork.

Playing a musical instrument

Emotional and social development

- have a growing sensitivity and begin to realise that others experience feelings of anger, fear and sadness similar to their own

- are easily embarrassed

- become discouraged easily

- take pride in their competence

- can be argumentative and bossy, but equally can be generous and responsive

- are beginning to see things from another's point of view, but still have trouble fully understanding the feelings and needs of other people

- form friendships quite casually and may change them very rapidly; friends are still primarily of the same gender, although they are beginning to show interest in the opposite sex

- like to belong to informal 'clubs' formed by children themselves; also like to belong to more structured adult-led groups, such as Cubs or Brownies

- begin to display a sense of loyalty to a group

- enjoy secrets and jokes.

Friends are still usually of the same gender

Children aged 10 and 11 years:

- show an increasing ability to understand the needs and opinions of others
- can identify and label or describe what they are feeling
- become increasingly self-conscious
- usually have a 'best friend' and may form more intense, longer-lasting friendships on the basis of a variety of shared interests and things in common
- may be experiencing sudden, dramatic, emotional changes associated with puberty (especially girls, who experience puberty earlier than boys)
- have a more defined personality – their idea of self being partly defined by the school environment
- tend to be particularly sensitive to criticism
- prefer to spend leisure time with friends and continue to belong to small groups of the same sex
- are acutely aware of the opposite sex
- succumb to peer pressure more readily and want to talk, dress and act just like friends
- become self-absorbed and introspective
- are more independent but still like adults to be present to help them.

Moral and spiritual development

Children aged 8 and 9 years:

- continue to think that rules are permanent and unchangeable because they are made up by adults who must be obeyed and respected
- have a clear idea of the difference between reality and fantasy, and are developing their own personal standards of right and wrong
- are highly concerned with fairness.

- understand that certain rules can be changed by mutual negotiation and that they are not always imposed by external authority; often, they do not accept rules that they did not help make

- begin to experience conflict between parents' values and those of their peers.

Play

Children need play just as much at this stage of development as they do earlier. By encouraging play both in and away from school, adults can give children the opportunities to interact with their peers and to learn about their environment from first-hand experience.

Children:
- enjoy co-operative and competitive games

- are very active and love being outdoors; physical exercise is vital for developing muscle strength

- enjoy traditional board games such as draughts and chess, word games, card games and quiz-type games, as well as the more complex fantasy games

- enjoy craft activities and making things from construction kits.

Safety when using the Internet

ICT *Guidelines for Children aged eight to twelve years*

Adult supervision and advice are essential both at home and at school. Parents need to set boundaries for computer and Internet use – for example:

- when and how long they can be on-line

- which areas of the worldwide web are appropriate to visit (favourite sites can be bookmarked to provide easy access)

- being in the same room when a young child uses the computer, or keeping the computer in an area where other family members are usually present; this will help to promote interaction and technological expertise.

See also page 129 for Safety when using the Internet

Promoting development

- Encourage children to take part in physical activities – such as dance, yoga and gymnastics.

- Encourage children to collect things such as shells, stamps or flowers.

- Encourage pretend play, because it still provides an important learning experience.

- Make time for running, hopping, skipping, jumping and climbing.

- Encourage children to dance or skip to music.

- Encourage children to talk about their feelings while working or playing together.

- Provide opportunities for practising life skills, for example cooking, sewing and designing dramatic play props.

- Provide time and space for a child to be alone. Time to read, daydream or do schoolwork uninterrupted will be appreciated.

- Teach basic social rules – how to share and co-operate, not to snatch things or shout at people.

- Find local activities where children have opportunities to make friends outside school such as Cubs, a drama group or swimming lessons.

SafetyPoints

Children should be taught to play sports in appropriate, safe, supervised areas, with proper equipment and rules – e.g. helmets and knee and elbow pads for cycling and for skateboarding.

Swimming and water safety lessons can prevent drowning.

Safety instruction regarding matches, fires, lighters, barbecues, campfires, and cooking on stoves or open fires can prevent major burns.

Make sure you – or another responsible adult – always know where the child is. Establish clear rules that they must come and tell you or contact you before moving on somewhere else.

Wearing seat belts remains the most important way of preventing major injury or death on the roads.

Twelve to sixteen years

A dolescence involves intense physical, emotional and psychological changes, with a huge variation in what is considered 'normal'. During this time adolescents move away from parental influence and become more independent. Peer groups tend to be mixed gender and gradually give way to one-to-one friendships and romances. There is often increasing conflict between adolescents and their parents. Young people are beginning to develop a social conscience, becoming concerned about social issues such as racism, global warming and poverty.

Physical development

Physical development in an adolescent is more commonly referred to as **puberty**. Puberty is the stage of growth in which a child's body turns into that of an adult. The child or young person undergoes physical, hormonal and sexual changes, and becomes capable of reproduction. They also experience a **growth spurt**, which involves rapid growth of bones and muscles. This begins in girls around the ages of 9–12 and in boys around the ages of 11–14.

The charts on the following pages detail the many physical changes that take place during puberty.

Puberty

The physical changes of adolescence are known as puberty. In both boys and girls, puberty starts with the release of hormones from the **pituitary gland** – a tiny gland located in the brain. **Hormones** are chemical messengers which allow different parts of the body to communicate with each other. In girls, the pituitary gland sends a message to the **ovaries** to start releasing another hormone called **oestrogen**. In boys, it sends a message to the **testicles** to start producing the hormone called **testosterone**. These two hormones are responsible for many of the changes associated with puberty. The age at which puberty starts varies from person to person, but on average it begins between 9–13 in girls and 10–15 in boys.

During puberty, many physical changes occur:

- Growth accelerates rapidly – often called a **growth spurt**. This usually happens in a particular order:
  - the head, feet and hands grow to adult size first; then
  - the arms and legs grow in length and strength; finally
  - the trunk, the main part of the body from shoulder to hip, grows to full adult size and shape.

This sequence of growth means that for a brief period, adolescents may feel gawky and clumsy, as they appear to be 'out of proportion'. The average boy grows fastest between 14 and 15; girls start earlier, growing fastest when 12 and 13. Girls also finish their growth spurt earlier, at 18, while boys need another two years before they finish growing at 20.

- **Secondary sexual characteristics** develop. These are external traits which distinguish the two sexes, but which are not directly part of the reproductive system; for example, the growth of pubic hair in both sexes, facial hair and deepened voice for males, and breasts and widened hips for females.

- **Primary sexual characteristics** develop. These are the penis and sperm in males and the vagina and ovaries in females. During puberty hormonal changes cause a boy's penis and testicles to grow and the body to produce sperm. Girls start to menstruate or have their monthly period. Both these events signal **sexual maturity** – the ability to reproduce.

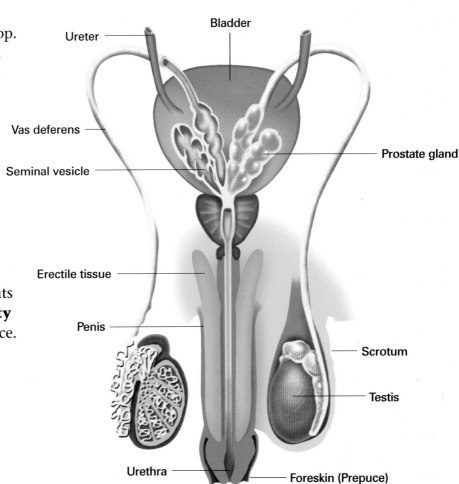

The male reproductive organs

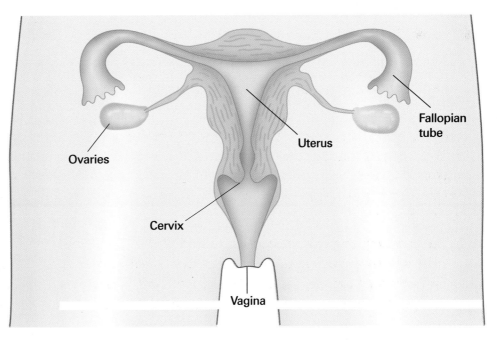

The female reproductive organs

A summary of physical development in puberty

In girls	In boys

In girls

The first *external* sign of puberty in most girls is usually breast development – often accompanied by a growth spurt.

Breasts develop At first, the nipples start to stick out from the chest. (often called 'budding'). Behind the nipple, milk ducts begin to grow. Next, the flat circular part of the nipple, the **areola**, rises and starts to expand. Glands that make sweat and scent develop beneath it. The breast begins to fill out, as fat is deposited around the nipple. Some girls feel a tingling sensation or have tender breasts. Initially the breasts stick out in a conical shape. As growth continues they gradually round off into an adult shape.

Body size and shape Grows taller. Hips widen as the pelvic bones grow. Fat develops on the hips, thighs and buttocks and the ratio of fat to muscle increases. The waist gets smaller and the body develops a more curved shape.

Menstruation Having periods is part of the female reproductive cycle which starts when girls become sexually mature during puberty. During a menstrual period, a woman bleeds from her uterus (womb) via the vagina. This lasts anything from three to seven days. Each period begins approximately every 28 days if the woman does not become pregnant during a given cycle. The onset of menstruation is called the **menarche**, and it can occur at any time between the ages of 9 and 16, most commonly around the age of 12–13.

In boys

The first *external* sign of puberty in most boys is an increase in the size of the testicles and then the penis. This is followed by the growth of pubic and underarm hair. At the same time, the voice deepens and muscles develop. Lastly, boys grow facial hair.

Voice breaking Testosterone causes the voice box – or larynx – to enlarge and the vocal cords to become longer. Sometimes, as the voice changes to become deeper, it may change pitch abruptly or 'break' at times; the voice box tilts and often protrudes at the neck – as an 'Adam's apple'.

Many boys start to develop **breasts** in their teenage years, but these disappear as the testosterone levels increase.

Body size and shape Grows taller. Body takes on a new, more muscular shape as the shoulders and chest become broader and the neck becomes more muscular.

Chest hair may appear during puberty – or some years later.

Penile erections These occur spontaneously even from infancy, but during puberty they become more frequent. Erections can occur with or without any physical or sexual stimulation and can cause acute embarrassment.

Sperm Once the testicles begin to grow they also develop their adult function – producing sperm. Mature sperm is present in the male body towards the end of puberty (most commonly between the ages of 13 and 15), and means that the body is capable of reproduction.

Pubic hair This starts to grow around the genitals and becomes coarse, dark and curly. In girls, pubic hair forms an upside-down triangle shape; in boys, the hair grows between the legs and extends up from the penis to the abdomen.

Hair grows in the armpits and on the legs.

Sweat A different kind of sweat is now produced in response to stress, emotion and sexual excitement. It is produced by the apocrine glands and only occurs in the armpits, the belly button, the groin area, the ears and the nipples. As bacteria break down the sweat it starts to smell strongly – known as B.O. (Body Odour).

Oil glands Oil-secreting glands in the skin can become over-active – this can cause skin to become greasier and can also cause acne.

Cognitive and language development

Adolescents:
- experience a major shift in thinking from the concrete to the abstract – an adult way of thinking*; this involves:

  - *thinking about possibilities:* whereas younger children rely heavily on their senses to apply reasoning, adolescents think about possibilities that are not directly observable

  - *thinking ahead:* young people start to plan ahead, often in a systematic way; younger children may, for example, look forward to a holiday, but are unlikely to focus on the preparation involved

  - *thinking through hypotheses:* this gives them the ability to make and test hypotheses and to think about situations that are contrary to fact

  - *thinking about their own thought processes:* this is known as **metacognition**; a subcategory of metacognition is metamemory, which is having knowledge about your memory processes – being able to explain what strategies you use when trying to remember things, such as for an exam.

  - *thinking beyond conventional limits:* thinking about issues that generally preoccupy human beings in adulthood, such as morality, religion and politics

- approach a problem in a systematic fashion

- use imagination when solving problems

- have a fast, legible style of handwriting.

* **Piaget** described this as the **formal operational stage** of cognitive development (see *Theories of Development,* page 157)

Emotional and social development

Socially, adolescence is characterised by an increasing independence from parents. Young people undergo several transitions – making their own decisions, testing the limits of authority, forming sexual partnerships and preparing to complete their education or to leave home.

Adolescents:

- may alternate between behaving like a child and behaving as an adult, depending on the stage of physical development

- may become self-conscious or anxious about their physical changes (too short, too tall, too fat, too thin etc.)

- develop a sexual identity; self-labelling as gay or lesbian tends to occur around the age of 15 for boys and 15½ for girls, although first disclosure does not normally take place until after the age of 16½ years for both sexes

- often feel misunderstood

- can experience wide emotional swings, for example fluctuate between emotional peaks of excitement and depths of moodiness

- want to be accepted and liked

- tend to identify more with friends and begin to separate from parents; they are less dependent on family for affection and emotional support

- seek recognition from their peers; their peer group influences interests and clothing styles

- become more socially skilled and better at resolving conflicts

- become more introspective; this examination of their inner experiences may include writing a diary.

Resolving conflicts with friends

Moral and spiritual development

Adolescents:
- are able to think beyond themselves more and to understand the perspective of another
- develop their own ideas and values which often challenge those of their parents
- may deliberately flout rules or keep to them only if there is otherwise a risk of being caught.

Promoting development

- Encourage plenty of physical activity. Exercise will help young people burn off excess energy, strengthen developing muscles and sleep better at night. It may also help them become more comfortable in their changing bodies.

- Encourage them to get enough sleep. The growth hormone is released principally at night during sleep, with short bursts every one to two hours during the deep-sleep phase. Young people who are consistently deprived of sleep during puberty are smaller than they should be.

- Encourage healthy eating habits. During adolescence, young people need to take in more calories to fuel their rapid growth. (*See* Nutrition Guidelines, page 129.)

- Provide honest answers to questions about sex.

- Never criticise their appearance. Adolescents often spend large amounts of time grooming themselves and obsessing over skin-care products. Acne can be a major concern.

- Be understanding of their need for physical space. They may withdraw from physical affection with family members during this period; maintain communication, but respect their need for personal space.

- Create opportunities for them to challenge their thinking skills, using brain-teasers and other puzzles.

- Help them research solutions and learn about the history or background to a problem.

- Encourage reading – for study and for pleasure.

- Allow plenty of time for peer interaction.

- Provide opportunities for leadership skills – for example, helping to teach younger children.

- Encourage them to take an active part in setting rules and boundaries, such as what time they are expected to return home in the evening.

Chapter 16 Twelve to sixteen years

- Listen to their ideas and show respect for them; try to involve them in discussing their behavioural rules and consequences.

- Provide opportunities for participation in *controlled* risky activities, for example involvement in (properly supervised) sports, such as parachuting or rock climbing.

- Provide opportunities for involvement in community activities, for example volunteering at a homeless shelter or a day centre for disabled people.

- Talk to them about their views and encourage debate. Find out what they think about news stories on television or in the paper; ask them about their political and spiritual beliefs.

- Encourage involvement in projects or activities both within school and after school. At the same time, encourage them to stick with a project or activity long enough to establish some skills.

- Praise them for their efforts as well as their abilities. This will help them to persevere with activities instead of giving up if they are not immediately successful.

- Help them to explore career goals and options. Set up opportunities for them to 'job shadow' others. It is important for them to find out what they *don't* like doing, as well as what they enjoy.

Playing pool together

Safety when using the Internet

Although the risk of encountering a child sexual offender *on-line* is thought to be small, children should be taught the safety lessons of the Internet. These guidelines apply to anyone who uses the Internet to chat on-line:

Stay safe Keep personal information safe by *never* giving it out to strangers. Also never give away friends' details on-line – their street addresses, email addresses, mobile numbers or anything that could identify them off-line. Keep any Internet passwords secret too.

Meeting Never meet up with someone you have only met in a chat room, no matter how long you've known them and how tempting it seems.

Emails Watch out for emails from people unknown to you. Never accept these or open any attachments.

Be wary of lies It's easy to lie on-line: people may not be who they say they are. Child sex offenders often pretend to be the same age as the child or a little older.

Chat rooms Stick to public chat rooms; most have an 'alert' button you can press if you feel concerned about another chatter's behaviour, or you could keep a record of worrying conversations by hitting 'print screen'. Never say anything in a chat room that you wouldn't say in public. Remember, you are in control and can leave a chat room or log off at any time.

Tell someone Tell a parent, carer or teacher if you ever feel uncomfortable about anything you see on the Internet.

Health education

Many health education topics are now addressed in secondary schools, but there is still a real problem with teenage pregnancies, sexually transmitted diseases (STDs) and alcohol abuse. Adolescents need clear, non-judgemental information about:

- making safe decisions about relationships, sexual intercourse and how to stand up for their decisions
- resisting pressures from friends or others for unwanted sex or drugs
- how to recognise and avoid or leave a situation that may be risky or turn violent
- finding out where friendly local youth services are and how to access them
- how to ensure they have safer sex
- the risks to health and safety from drinking too much alcohol.

Healthy eating

Young people in this age group are growing fast and they need an increase in food to supply the energy they need for growth. They need more calories than adults, but the sort of food that is best is the same as for anyone else (see Healthy eating plan, page 112). Approximately half of all calories should come from complex carbohydrates such as cereals, pasta, rice and bread, and from root and leaf vegetables and fruit. About a third of calories should come from foods such as chicken, meat, oily fish, milk, cheese, eggs and yogurt. The rest will be made up of other foods such as fats.

Eating more than our bodies need means we put on weight. So to keep a healthy weight it's important to follow a balanced diet and keep physically active. Some dairy products are high in saturated fat and so should only be eaten in small amounts, or less often. The table below gives some ideas to help in following a healthy eating plan.

Foods to avoid or use sparingly	Reason	Choose instead	Why?
Fizzy drinks	High in sugar and acid – cause damage to tooth enamel and increase tooth decay	Plain or flavoured milks or yoghurt drinks	Good for strengthening bone and preventing fractures during sport
'Diet' or low calorie soft drinks	High in acid which dissolves tooth enamel	Plain or sparkling water	Very teeth-friendly and good for hydrating the skin
Crisps and other savoury snacks	High in saturated fat and salt	Sandwiches with meat, fish, egg or hummus and salad fillings	More protein, iron and zinc for skin repair and building up muscle rather than fat
Croissants, doughnuts, sweet pastries, flapjacks	Very high in fat	Hot cross buns, tea bread, fruit scones	Good for an energy boost with less fat. Also have more vitamins for good skin repair
Thin fries	Very high in fat	Chunky oven chips	Less fat and fewer calories
Burger and fries	Very high in fat	Burger in bun without the fries	More protein for skin repair and muscle building
Fried rice and fried noodles	Extra fat	Boiled or steamed rice or noodles	Good for vitamins without fat
Creamy and oily sauces with pasta	High in fat with few nutrients	Tomato-based or vegetable sauces with pasta	More vitamins and antioxidants in the vegetables for skin repair
Any meat or fish fried in batter	The batter coatings are high in fat with few nutrients	Eat the chicken or fish but avoid eating most of the batter	Protein, iron, zinc and B vitamins from the meat or fish are good for muscle building

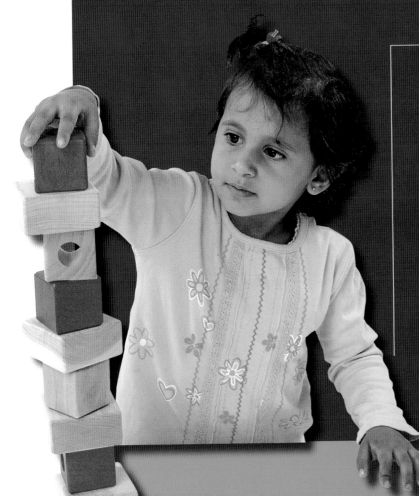

Chapter 17

Developmental assessment

This section looks briefly at the standard developmental assessments carried out on children from birth to the age of 5. After the age of 5, the school health service takes over the assessments.

If a child has a developmental delay, carers will want to know about the problem as soon as possible: it is easier to come to terms with a serious problem in a young baby than in an older child.

Health professionals should always take carers' concerns seriously and must never treat parents or other carers as fussy, neurotic or over-anxious.

Section **2**

Parent-held records

In most clinics carers are given a personal child health record or a similar document to keep for their baby. This is a way of keeping track of the child's progress.

Records are kept of the child's:

- height and weight
- immunisations
- childhood illnesses and accidents.

Development reviews

Regular development reviews are carried out in child health clinics and at the child's home by general practitioners, health visitors and school nurses. If the child's first language is not English, development reviews can be carried out with the help of someone who can speak the child's language.

Children's holistic development is reviewed as:

- gross motor skills: sitting, standing, walking, running
- fine motor skills: handling toys, stacking bricks, doing up buttons and tying shoelaces (gross and fine manipulative skills)
- speech and language, including hearing
- vision
- social behaviour.

Reviews give carers opportunities to say what they have noticed about their child. They can also discuss anything that concerns them about their child's health and behaviour.

Ages for reviews

Note that in some parts of the country, especially after the age of 3, the ages at which children are reviewed may vary slightly from those given below.

Shortly after birth, the newborn baby is examined by a **paediatrician** or family doctor. Specific checks are made to assess the development of the baby:

- the baby is weighed

- the spine is checked for any evidence of **spina bifida**

- the mouth is checked for evidence of a **cleft palate** – a gap in the roof of the mouth

- the head is checked for size and shape, and the head circumference is measured

- the eyes are checked for **cataracts**

- the neck is examined for any obvious injury to the neck muscles after a difficult birth

- the hands are checked for webbing (fingers joined together at the base) or creases (a single unbroken crease from one side of the palm to the other is one feature of **Down's syndrome**)

- the hips are tested for congenital dislocation

- the feet are checked for webbing and **talipes** (club foot)

- the reflex actions are observed (see pages 8 and 9)

- the hearing is tested, often by means of **Otoacoustic Emissions Testing** (OAE) or the 'cradle test': this involves placing a sponge earphone into the ear canal, then stimulating the ear with sound and measuring an 'echo' – the echo is found in all normal-hearing individuals, so its absence may indicate a hearing loss and the need for further testing.

Other medical checks include:

- listening to the heart and lungs to detect any abnormality

- examining the anus and the genitalia for any malformation.

A newborn baby

Developmental reviews from 6 weeks onwards are conducted under these headings: 'Discussion', 'Observation', 'Measurement' and 'Examination'.

Discussion

Carers are asked if they have any general concerns about their baby, in particular about:

- feeding
- sleeping
- bowel actions and passing urine.

They are also asked whether they think that the baby can:

- hear – for example, does the baby 'startle' at a sudden noise?
- see – for example, does the baby turn her or his head to follow the carer?

Observation

While the carer is undressing the baby for examination, the doctor will look out for:

- the responsiveness of the baby – smiles, eye contact, attentiveness to the carer's voice and so on
- any difficulties the carer has in holding the baby, for example a depressed mother will lack visual attention and may not hold and support the baby adequately
- any signs of jaundice or anaemia.

This is also an opportunity to provide help and support to the baby's main carers.

Measurement

The baby is weighed naked and the weight plotted on a **growth (centile) chart**.

The head circumference is measured and plotted on the growth chart.

Responding to the main carer

Examination

The general appearance of the baby will indicate general health and whether he or she is well nourished.

In addition:

- the eyes are inspected using a light – babies will turn their head and follow a small light beam

- the heart and hips are checked again

- the baby is placed in the prone position, in which he or she will turn the head to one side, and hold the hands with the thumbs inwards and the fingers wrapped around them

- the **posterior fontanelle** is usually closed by now; the **anterior fontanelle** does not close until around 18 months.

Assessment at 6–9 months

Discussion

Carers are asked whether they have any concerns about their baby's health and development.

Observation

The doctor will note:

- **socialisation** and **attachment** behaviour, particularly how the baby interacts with the carer – most babies are clingy at this age

- **communication** – sounds, expression and gestures

- **motor development** – sitting, balance, use of hands, any abnormal movement patterns.

While the baby is sitting on the carer's lap, the doctor will also observe the baby's muscle tone.

Measurement

The baby's head circumference and weight are measured and plotted on the growth chart.

Examination

The following checks are made:

Baby using both hands equally

- the hips are checked by manipulation

- the heart and lungs are examined by listening

- in boys, the testes are examined

- the baby's vision will be observed for any signs of a squint

- the baby's grasp is assessed: when offered a toy a baby will usually take it with one hand and pass it to the other – the baby is observed for equal use of both hands and accuracy in grasping and passing

- the baby's pincer grasp will be assessed: some babies can use a pincer grasp to pick up tiny 'hundreds and thousands' sweets, which are usually taken straight to the mouth and can be safely eaten

- hearing may be tested: if any abnormality is detected the baby will be referred to an audiologist (a hearing specialist).

Assessment at 18–24 months

Discussion

Carers are asked if they have any general concerns about their child's development, and particularly with the child's vision, speech and hearing. If there is a problem, the child may be referred to a specialist.

The doctor will ask about behaviour, including any problems such as temper tantrums, sleep disturbance, poor appetite or food fads. Iron deficiency is sometimes a problem at this age and may be a cause of irritability and behavioural problems as well as anaemia.

For boys, the carer is asked if the testes are present in the scrotal sac. If they are not, the doctor will examine the child and refer him to a specialist.

Observation

The child is observed walking to check whether the gait is normal.

Measurement

If the child is co-operative, height is measured.

Weight is measured only if there is a cause for concern.

Examination

Manipulation skills are checked – can the child:

- build a tower of six or seven cubes?
- hold a pencil using a thumb and two fingers?
- turn the pages of a book singly?

Holding a crayon, demonstrating manipulative skills

Assessment at 4–5 years

Discussion

Carers are asked if they have any general concerns about the child's development or about emotional or behavioural problems.

The doctor will also be concerned with the child's ability to concentrate, to play with others and to separate from the main carer without distress.

Observation

Motor skills are checked:

- can the child walk, run and climb stairs?
- does the child tire more quickly than other children?

Fine manipulative skills are checked:

- can the child control pencils and paint brushes?
- can the child draw a cross?

Hopping, demonstrating motor skills

Drawing a cross, demonstrating fine manipulative skills

Vision, language and hearing are also assessed, by observation and by discussion with the carers. If there are any particular problems, specialist assessment can be arranged.

Measurement

Height and weight are measured and plotted on the growth chart.

Examination

Other checks will depend on any concerns that the carer or the doctor may have. For example, if the child has asthma an examination of the lungs may take place.

The school health team continues to monitor the health and development of all schoolchildren up to the age of 16. Teachers and other education professionals may refer any pupil for assessment, and school nurses are increasingly involved in health education programmes within schools.

Chapter 18

Children with special needs

The term 'special needs' is used to describe children whose development differs from the norm.

Like that of all other children, the development of children with special needs is influenced by:

- the quality of their experiences
- the quality of their social relationships
- the learning opportunities they are offered.

Sometimes the special need is identified before birth or soon after. Other special needs, such as a heart disorder or a visual or hearing impairment, may become apparent only much later.

What are special needs?

Children with special needs are not an easily defined group. Some have a very obvious and well-researched disability, such as Down's syndrome or **cerebral palsy**; others may have a specific learning difficulty such as **dyslexia** or **giftedness**. What defines them as children with special needs is the fact that they need *additional help* in some areas of development when compared with other children.

It is important to remember that children are more alike than different. Children with disabilities share the same basic needs as other children, but the disabilities may affect the meeting of those needs or create additional needs. Thus a child who lacks speech may find it difficult to communicate needs or make friends and a child who lacks mobility may be isolated by not being able to join in the activities of others. Children need to feel welcome and they need to feel safe, both physically and emotionally. They also need to have friends and to feel that they belong. All children should be encouraged to live up to their potential, and every child should be celebrated for his or her uniqueness. Always look at children as individuals first, and *then* consider their special needs.

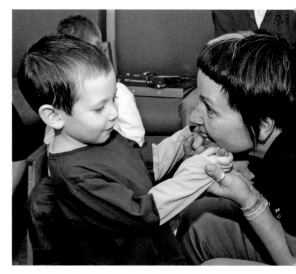

Encouraging participation in a group activity

Kinds of special need

Special needs may be grouped into the following categories:

- *physical impairment* – needs related to problems with mobility or co-ordination, and sometimes **dyspraxia**

- *sensory impairment* – needs related to problems with sight or hearing

- *speech or language difficulties* – needs related to problems such as delayed language, difficulties in articulation or stuttering

- *moderate to severe learning disabilities* – needs related to problems many of which result from a genetic defect or from an accident or a trauma

- *specific learning difficulties* (SLD) – needs related to problems with the areas of reading, writing or numeracy (usually)

- *a medical condition* – needs related to conditions such as asthma, cystic fibrosis or diabetes

- *emotional difficulties* – needs related to conditions such as anxiety, fear, depression, **autism**

- *behavioural difficulties* – needs related to aggression, **attention deficit hyperactivity disorder** (**ADHD**), or antisocial behaviour

- *giftedness* – needs related to being highly gifted, academically or artistically.

Some children may have a special need at a particular time only, such as when a parent or sibling has died, or when they have been a victim of bullying or abuse.

Inclusive care and education

Children have special educational needs if they have a learning difficulty that calls for extra support. (The words 'special educational needs' are often shortened to 'SEN'.) A child may also develop special needs as the result of an accident or illness – for example, **meningitis** can cause sensory impairments.

A learning difficulty means that the child finds it more difficult to learn than most other children of the same age, or has a disability that makes it difficult for her or him to use ordinary school facilities. One in five children may have special educational needs at some stage during their education. These may be apparent at a very early age or may develop later.

The Children Act 2004 promotes the integration of disabled children in mainstream settings, such as nursery schools, day nurseries, schools and family centres. This approach is called **inclusive care and education**, and recognises that care and education are inextricably linked.

Providing for children with special needs

Child development centres

In some areas, teams of professionals – doctors, therapists, health visitors and social workers – are available to help support children with special needs and their families. Usually such teams work from what is known as a child development centre. Parents can be referred to this service by their general practitioner or health visitor.

Many services are available to help children who have special needs to learn and develop. For example:

- *physiotherapy*

- *speech and language therapy*

- *occupational therapy*

- *home learning schemes* – for example, the Portage scheme provides trained home visitors to work with parents and their young children

A physiotherapy session

- *equipment and special aids* provisions, such as pushchairs, wheelchairs, communication aids or hearing aids

- *financial support* to help families where children need help with personal care and/or mobility

- *toy libraries* – most areas have a toy library for children with special needs from which specially chosen toys can be borrowed for use at home

- *specialist playgroups, opportunity groups and children's centres* – these centres often provide on-site physiotherapy, nursing care and play therapy

- *respite care* – for instance, Crossroads, a national voluntary organisation that provides trained care assistants for the practical respite care needed by some children with disabilities

- *playgroups* – state-run, privately run or voluntary

- *nurseries, school nurseries* and *classes*.

To find out what's available in your area, ask your health visitor, your GP, the social services department or the educational adviser for special needs at your local education department.

Promoting development in children with special needs

Many children with special needs who attend mainstream nurseries and schools will require one-to-one attention from a trained early years worker. The following section provides some ideas for those working with children with special needs.

Children with physical impairments

Children with physical limitations have specific needs depending on their particular disability.

Friends and classmates are usually eager to assist a child with a physical difficulty. Although such helpful behaviour should be applauded, children with physical problems also need encouragement to do as much as possible for themselves. This may mean that tasks and chores take a little more time, but being patient and encouraging promotes self-confidence and independence.

▶ Difficulties

Children who have difficulties with gross motor skills:

- may stumble and trip frequently
- may have difficulty walking or running, jumping or climbing, or be unable to do these at all
- may have poor balance
- may have difficulty in bouncing, catching or throwing balls
- may be unable to release objects voluntarily.

Children who have difficulties with fine motor skills:

- may have poorly developed hand or finger co-ordination
- may have difficulty in picking up small objects
- may have difficulty in drawing or writing.

Throwing bean bags promotes physical development and co-ordination skills

Make sure that the environment is suitable:

- Check that doors are wide enough, that door handles can be reached and that toileting facilities are accessible.

- Provide heavy, stable furniture and equipment that are not easily knocked over.

- Avoid rugs. Arrange furniture and equipment to allow for a wide pathway for users of walking frames or wheelchairs.

- Provide a safe place to store walkers, crutches, sticks or canes so that other children do not trip over them.

Provide suitable equipment:

- Provide objects that can be used for grasping, holding, transferring and releasing. Make sure that the object is appropriate for the child's age – for instance, a bean bag made from dinosaur fabric is much more appropriate for a 5-year-old than a rattle or baby toy.

- Work with parents and carers to find comfortable ways for children to sit. For example, one child may like a corner with two walls for support, another may need a chair with a seat belt or a wheelchair with a large tray across the arms.

- Make objects as steady as possible. For instance, fix paper, mixing bowls or wood blocks to the table or floor with tape so that they remain secure when the child is painting, drawing, stirring or hammering.

- Provide materials of different textures – such as play dough, fabric swatches, ribbon, corrugated cardboard and sandpaper – to encourage the sense of touch.

Using a gym ball to encourage exercise

Offer appropriate activities:

- Plan activities to encourage exercise and movement of all body parts.

- Work with parents or carers and specialists to give special exercises for children, depending on each child's individual needs.

Most children who are considered visually impaired do have some usable vision. Even those considered blind are often able to tell the difference between light and dark.

Children with visual impairment are frequently delayed in their physical and motor skills; for example, they may not be able to locate or pick up small objects they have dropped. Helping children understand about space and size will help to promote their development.

▶ Difficulties

Children:

- may sometimes or always cross one or both eyes
- may have eyes that won't focus
- may blink or rub their eyes a lot
- may tilt their head to the side or the front
- may squint or frown a great deal
- may be unable to locate and pick up small objects that have been dropped
- may turn their face away when being addressed, if they are using some peripheral vision
- may hold books or objects very close to their face
- may avoid bright lights
- may stumble or fall a great deal, or trip over small objects
- may cover one eye
- may appear inattentive
- may complain of dizziness, a headache or nausea after doing intense work.

▶ Promoting development

Make sure that the environment is suitable:

- Provide cues – during dressing, eating or any other daily activity, communicate clearly so that the child knows what will be happening.
- Avoid sudden changes of lighting. For example, when a child is to move from a darker hallway to a bright playroom, you could partially close the blinds before the child enters the playroom, and open them again after a few minutes when the eyes have had time to adjust.
- Keep cupboard doors fully open or fully closed. Pad table corners. Make sure there are no curled-up edges on rugs.

- Always keep furniture in the same place, so that the child can use it as a guide around the room.

- Keep toys, personal items and the potty-chair within easy reach.

Provide suitable equipment:

- Offer babies objects for play that have hard, shiny surfaces – visually impaired babies often find furry objects off-putting.

Enjoying cause and effect in the sensory room

- Using an adult-sized toilet may make a young child with a visual impairment feel insecure. A small potty-chair might be more comfortable because the child can feel the floor underfoot and get on and off the potty-chair without help.

- Use carefully chosen clues – sounds, textures, scents or highly visible objects – to help children move around the nursery more confidently. For example, you could have wind chimes on one door, and different floor textures in different areas.

- Look for toys and books with raised numerals, letters or designs that children can touch and explore.

- Cut out symbols, shapes, letters and numbers from sandpaper or cardboard. Guide the child's hand over these shapes as you discuss them.

Using a mirror and lights to promote visual co-ordination

Offer appropriate activities:

- Take babies around the house and name the sound clues they hear, such as a ticking clock or a wind chime.

- Don't be too quick to 'rescue' children. Try to give them the *least* assistance possible. Rather than rush to their aid, always ask children if they need help.

- Ask carers whether their child likes to be touched. Some children with visual impairments don't, but most do. A simple touch on the shoulder can be very reassuring.

- Use language full of descriptions. Tell children about colours, the weather and things that are happening around them. This may seem awkward at first, but you will get used to it.

- Use names. A child with a visual impairment may not be able to see the facial expressions or body language that show others which person is being spoken to such as which child you have turned your head towards; speak to each child by name, especially when there are other people in the room.

- Use your voice to communicate feelings and meaning. Tone and volume can communicate sadness, happiness, anger or other emotions.

- Relate directions to body parts. Rather than say 'You dropped your mitten on the floor' say instead, 'You dropped your mitten on the floor in front of your right foot'.

- Tell children when you are leaving them. Encourage other children to do the same; they will learn quickly by example.

- Provide activities with sensory experiences. Children with visual impairment learn through hearing and touch. Sand and water play, collages, play dough and finger-painting are good learning activities.

- Follow up descriptions with concrete experiences. For example, after reading the story of 'The Three Little Pigs', the child might find it interesting to feel the difference between straw, sticks and bricks.

- Teach non-disabled children to identify themselves to children with visual disabilities, and to describe their art activities or building constructions in words.

- Encourage children to build horizontally with blocks. Children can feel shapes and lay blocks end to end or in different patterns without the frustration of falling blocks.

Children who have difficulty hearing need opportunities to learn how to listen and speak. Provide activities that encourage communication and language development. Children can develop important language skills with practice. Activities with very little verbal interaction are also very important.

▶ Difficulties

Children:

- may not respond when spoken to
- may not startle at a loud noise
- may not wake up in response to sound
- may talk but be impossible to understand
- may leave out many sounds when talking
- may seem unable to follow verbal directions
- may hold their head so that one ear is turned toward the speaker
- may talk in a very loud or a very soft voice
- may coo or gurgle, but may not progress to saying words
- may talk very little or not at all
- may talk in a monotone voice
- may interrupt conversations or seem unaware that others are talking
- may be alert and attentive to things that can be seen but not to those others would hear.

Playing with hand puppets promotes emotional and social development

Make sure that the environment is suitable:

- During activities, cut down on background noise from the radio and machines such as dishwashers. Use carpets, rugs and pillows to absorb excess sound.

- Provide children with visual cues. For example, label shelves with a picture of toys to make tidying away toys easier. Use pictures to illustrate the steps of a recipe during cooking activities.

- Make eye contact before you start to speak. A gentle tap on the shoulder will usually get a child's attention.

- Talk in a normal voice – do not shout. Use gestures and facial expressions to clarify your message.

Provide suitable equipment:

- Provide headphones, or set up a special area where a tape recorder can be played at a higher volume.

- Provide toys that make a lot of noise – children can feel the vibrations even when they cannot hear the sound.

- Find out how to look after hearing aids and how to protect them from loss or damage within the school or nursery – for example, sand and dirt can damage them.

Offer appropriate activities:

- Teach children to use gestures and sign language, for example **Signalong, Makaton** or **the Picture Exchange Communication System (PECS)**.

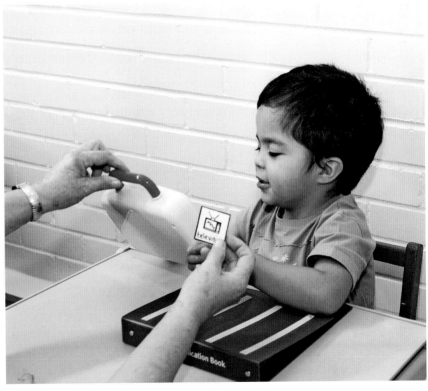

A structured activity using the Picture Exchange Communication System

- Encourage children to talk about what they are doing. Ask open-ended questions that require an answer; these will encourage the child to practise using language.

- Use stories, songs and finger-play to enhance language development.

- Repeat favourite rhymes and songs to encourage confidence in developing language skills.

- Encourage dancing to music: children will feel the vibrations and enjoy the chance to express themselves.

Children with learning disabilities

Children with learning disabilities will usually go through the typical sequence of developmental stages but at a much slower rate. Characteristics vary widely with different disabilities, but a few approaches can be applied to all.

◉ Difficulties

Children:

- may have a short attention span and be easily distracted

- may have difficulty in making transitions, such as from one class to the next

- may prefer to play with younger children

- may speak and use language like a much younger child

- may be afraid of trying new things

- may have difficulty in problem-solving

- may not remember things well

- may not be able to transfer learning to a new situation

- may repeat the same movement over and over again.

A soft playroom provides a safe area for physical exercise and play

Make sure that the environment is suitable:

- Keep verbal instructions simple.

- Tell children how to do something and show them by guiding their hands and body through the movements of an activity.

- Avoid sudden transitions. When it's time to end an activity or to move to another activity, give the child plenty of warning.

- Provide cues to help children know what is expected from them – for example, mark their coat hook with a picture of a child hanging up a coat.

- Expect appropriate behaviour – don't allow a child with a learning disability to behave in ways that are not allowed in other children.

- Provide opportunities to play near a child who is doing a similar activity. This can give the child with learning difficulties some ideas about how to use and explore the same materials.

Playing alongside another child promotes social development

Offer appropriate activities:

- Break activities into small steps and give one instruction at a time.

- Practise activities over and over again.

- Allow children plenty of time to practise new things that they are learning.

- Select activities that match the child's mental age and abilities.

- Try not to overwhelm the child with too many toys or art materials at once.

Provide suitable equipment:

- Make sure that there are obvious differences in size, shape and colour when sorting or classifying objects. Differences that are too subtle, such as between maroon and red, or oval shapes and circles, may be confusing.

Children with behavioural difficulties

Children with behavioural difficulties often display one of three types of extreme behaviour: withdrawal, aggression or hyperactivity. Each type of behaviour may require a different strategy to promote social and emotional development.

▶ Difficulties

Children:

- may use aggressive behaviour to deal with most situations
- may show extreme fear and anxiety
- may seem not to recognise basic feelings of happiness, sadness, anger or fear
- may always react in the same way, such as crying or hitting
- may not want to be touched
- may withdraw or stay quiet and passive most of the time
- may show excessive activity, restlessness or inability to stick to a task
- may regress to babyish behaviour whenever stress occurs
- may cry a great deal, seem depressed and unhappy, and seldom laugh.

▶ Promoting development

Make sure that the environment is suitable:

- Treat children uniquely. Always take them seriously, and show that you believe in them.
- Listen to each child with respect. Don't compare the child who is being aggressive with another child who is playing well.
- Invite a withdrawn child to join in an activity by watching others. As the child becomes more comfortable, demonstrate how to play with materials or toys. Encourage the child to play along with you.
- Watch for signs of aggressive behaviour and intervene quickly. Teach problem-solving skills.

Offer appropriate activities:

- Provide developmentally appropriate activities that are not overly difficult and which will help the child feel capable. Avoid activities that can be done in only one way.

- Watch for periods when children are less excitable and more in control. Use these times to present a new activity that requires some concentration.

- Keep stories and group activities short to match attention spans. Seat the child near you and away from distractions such as a nearby shelf of toys.

- Avoid over-stimulation. Limit the number of toys or materials you set out at one time.

- Provide adult guidance and structure. Help children to plan or to organise an activity. For example, if a child wants to play at being a firefighter you could suggest some props, such as a bucket and a blanket, and perhaps invite other children to play.

- Announce the tidying-up time and other transitions ahead of time. During the transition, give the child a specific task.

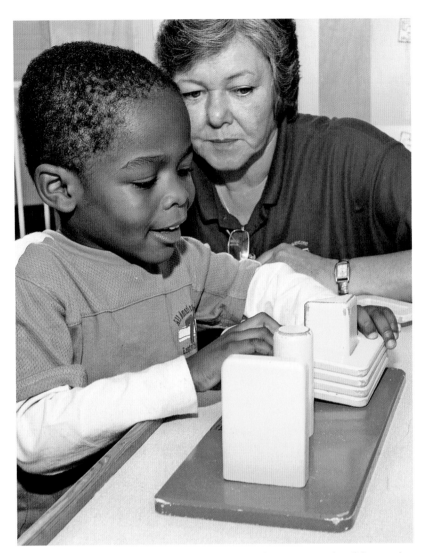

Helping a child to focus in a structured activity session

Special needs assessment

Local education authorities who think that children over 2 years old may have special educational needs must make an assessment of their needs. For children under 2, an assessment must be made if parents ask for it.

This assessment is a way of getting advice about the child's educational needs, and parents can take part in the assessment. The Advisory Centre for Education (page 175) offers advice and produces a handbook on the subject.

Voluntary organisations

There are many voluntary organisations that focus on particular disabilities and illnesses; these organisations are a valuable source of information, advice and support for parents and professionals. Through them, parents can often be put in touch with other parents in similar situations. Contact a Family (see page 175) is the national voluntary organisation that provides mutual support and advice for groups of families living in the same neighbourhood whose children have special needs.

Enjoying being part of a special group

Children with special needs – a checklist

The following questions can help parents and carers to ensure that they receive the help and support they need.

- Is there a name for my child's condition? If so, what is it?

- Are more tests needed to get a clear diagnosis or to confirm what has been found out?

- Is the condition likely to get worse, or will it stay roughly the same?

- Where is the best place to go for medical help?

- Where is the best place to go for practical help?

- How can I get in touch with other parents who have children with a similar condition?

- How can I find out how best to help my child?

Chapter 19

Theories of child development

M ost theories of child development rely to a great extent on the detailed observation of children in their own cultural contexts. Studying the way in which children think, learn, behave and feel therefore helps to advance our understanding of child development.

The following charts summarise the main theories of child development. The main theorists in each area of development are:

Cognitive development	Emotional and social development
Jean Piaget (1896–1980)	Sigmund Freud (1856–1939)
Lev Vygotsky (1896–1934)	E.H. Erikson (1902–1979)
Jerome Bruner (b. 1915)	John Bowlby (1907–1990)

Piaget, Bruner and **Vygotsky** all emphasised cognitive development as being closely linked to the brain's construction of knowledge within a *social* context.

- **Piaget** considered the most critical factor in a child's cognitive development to be interaction with peers; such interaction provides opportunities for the child to have cognitive conflict, which results in arguing or debating with peers. It also requires children to *decentre*, or consider another person's point of view. Piaget observes that children are most challenged in their thinking when they are with peers, because they all are on an equal footing and are freer to confront ideas than when interacting with adults.

- **Bruner** also observes that the process of constructing knowledge of the world is not done in isolation but rather within a social context. The child is a social being and, through social life, acquires a framework for interpreting experiences.

- **Vygotsky** believed that the most fruitful experience in a child's education is his or her collaboration with more skilled partners. He asserted that the more experienced partner provides help in the way of an intellectual scaffold, which allows the less experienced learner to accomplish more complex tasks than may be possible alone.

Freud, Erikson and **Bowlby** believed in the importance of detailed observations of children and of gaining close relationships with them.

- **Freud** constructed a stage theory of psychosexual development in children, who were said to be particularly sensitised at certain ages. He also warned that a person could become fixated at a particular stage, if their needs were not met.

- **Erikson** accepted Freud's stage theory, but also proposed that *psychosocial crises* beset individuals in adjusting to a particular social environment. His ideas influenced thinking about the development of **self-esteem** and the **self-concept**.

- **Bowlby** developed the **attachment theory**, based on his observations of the grief and despair of young children separated for long periods of time from the adult to whom they had become attached (usually their mothers); he concluded that attachment is vital to infants.

Piaget's theory of cognitive development

Age and stage	Characteristics
Birth to 2 years (approx.) **(Sensorimotor)**	Infants are developing their first **schemas**. They learn about themselves and their environment through sensation (sensori-) and movement (motor). There are six sub-stages in the sensorimotor stage: **1 Stage of reflex activity** (Birth to 1 month): grasping, sucking, eye movements, orientation to sound, etc. *Example*: Sucking to obtain milk; pressure on roof of mouth stimulates further sucking; and so on. **2 Stage of primary circular reactions** (1 to 4 months): Infant's behaviour, by chance, leads to an interesting result and is repeated. Circular = repetition; Primary = centred on infant's own body. *Example*: Thumb-sucking. **3 Stage of secondary circular reactions** (4 to 8 months): Repetition of simple actions on external objects. *Example:* Bangs a toy to make a noise. **4 Co-ordination of secondary circular reactions** (8 to 12 months): Combines actions to achieve a desired effect. The infant learns that he or she is separate from his or her environment and that aspects of his or her environment — parents or favourite toy – continue to exist even though they may be outside the reach of his or her senses; this is called **object permanence**. *Example*: Knocks a pillow away to reach for a desired toy. **5 Stage of tertiary circular reactions** (12 to 18 months): This involves the discovery of new means to meet goals: trial and error. Piaget describes the infant at this stage as the 'young scientist' – making early experiments. *Example*: An object hidden under one of several covers can be found. **6 Beginnings of symbolic representation** (18 to 24 months): Marks the beginnings of insight, or true creativity. The infant thinks about a problem before acting, and thoughts begin to dominate actions. This marks the passage into unique thought in the later three areas of development. *Example*: Searches for a hidden object, certain that it exists somewhere (the final stage of **object permanence**).
2 to 7 years (approx. **(Preoperational)**	Young children learn through their experiences with real objects in their immediate environment. Piaget subdivided this stage into: **1 Preconceptual substage** (2 to 4 years): Children are **egocentric**. They are unable to see or understand things from another person's viewpoint. **Symbolic functioning**: As language and fine motor skills develop, children use symbols (e.g. words and pictures) to make sense of their world. **2 Intuitive substage** (4 to 7 years): *Intuitive thought* occurs when the child is able to believe in something without knowing why she or he believes it. **Inability to conserve**: Through his conservation experiments (conservation of mass, volume and number) Piaget concluded that children in the preoperational stage will not be able to conserve mass, volume or number after the original form has changed. Also typical of this stage is **animism**. The child believes that all objects have some kind of consciousness. *Example*: A child may smack a chair if he collides with it and call it 'naughty chair'.
7 to 11 years (approx.) **(Concrete operational)**	Children continue to learn through their experiences with real objects. They are no longer subject to the illogical limitations of animism. Important processes during this stage are: **Decentring**: Children are less egocentric; they can increasingly see things from another's point of view and are able to concentrate on more than one thing at a time. **Reversibility**: The child understands that numbers or objects can be changed and then returned to their original state. *Example*: A child using play dough might explain: 'If I changed the cylinder shape back into a ball, it would be the same.' **Conservation:** Understanding that quantity, length or number of items is unrelated to the arrangement or appearance of the object or items. *Example*: When a child is presented with two equally sized, full cups they will be able to perceive that if water is transferred from one cup to a large jug it will **conserve** the quantity and be equal to the other filled cup. **Seriation**: The ability to arrange objects in an order according to size, shape or any other characteristic. *Example:* If given different-shaded objects they may make a colour gradient, from palest to darkest.

	Classification: The ability to name and identify sets of objects according to appearance, size or other characteristic, including the idea that one set of objects can include another. *Example*: A stamp collection organised first by country, then by picture identification (bird, flower etc.) and then perhaps by size or shape.
12 years to adult **(Formal operational)**	The main features of this stage are: **Abstract concepts**: Young people begin to develop a more abstract view of the world and can understand abstract concepts, such as fairness, justice and peace. **Deductive logic**: They understand that it is possible to create rules that help them to test things out, to have a hypothesis and to solve problems. **Combinational logic**: They can think in a rational, scientific manner and solve complex problems, e.g. algebraic formulas.

Conservation Skills	Basic Principles	Test for Conservation Skills	
		Step 1	**Step 2**
Number	The number of units in a collection remains unchanged even though they are arranged in space.	Two rows of buttons arranged in one-to-one correspondence	One of the rows elongated or contracted
Substance	The amount of a malleable, plastic-like material reamins unchanged regardless of the shape it assumes.	Modelling clay in two balls of the same size	One of the balls rolled into a long, narrow shape
Length	The length of a line or object from one end to the other end remains unchanged regardless of how it is rearranged in space or changed in shape.	Strips of cloth placed in a straight line	Strips of cloth placed in altered shapes
Area	The total amount of surface covered by a set of plane figures remains unchanged regardless of the position of the figures.	Square units arranged in a rectangle	Square units rearranged
Weight	The heaviness of an object remains unchanged regardless of the shape it assumes.	Units placed on top of each other	Units placed side by side

Bruner's theory of infant skill development

Bruner proposed that the usual course of intellectual development moves through three stages: enactive, iconic and symbolic, in that order. Unlike Piaget, Bruner did not state that these stages were necessarily age-dependent or inflexible. Bruner's theory has the following features:

Stage	Characteristics
Enactive stage	Knowledge is stored primarily in the form of **motor** responses. This applies to adults as well. Many adults can perform a variety of motor tasks (typing, sewing on a button, operating a lawn mower) that they would find difficult to describe in iconic (picture) or symbolic (word) form. Children need to have real, first-hand, direct experiences; this helps their thought processes to develop.
Iconic stage	Knowledge is stored primarily in the form of visual images. This may explain why, when we are learning a new subject, it is often helpful to have diagrams or illustrations to accompany verbal information. Children need to be reminded of their prior experiences; books and interest tables with objects laid out on them are useful aids to this recall of prior experiences.
Symbolic stage	Knowledge is stored primarily as words, mathematical symbols or in other symbol systems. According to Bruner's classification, these differ from icons in that symbols are 'arbitrary'. For example, the word *beauty* is an arbitrary designation for the idea of beauty in that the word itself is no more inherently beautiful than any other word. *Codes* are important: languages, music, mathematics, drawing, painting, dance and play are all useful codes which Bruner calls *symbolic thinking*.
Scaffolding	Adults can help develop children's thinking by being like a piece of scaffolding on a building. At first, the building has a great deal of scaffolding (i.e. adult support of the child's learning), but gradually, as the children extend their competence and control of the situation, the scaffolding is progressively removed until it is no longer needed. Scaffolding has particular features: • *Recruitment:* The teacher's first task is to engage the interest of the child and to encourage him or her to tackle the requirements of the task. • *Reduction of degrees of freedom:* The teacher has to simplify the task by reducing the number of actions required to reach a solution. The child needs to be able to see whether or not he or she achieved a fit with the task requirements. • *Direction maintenance:* The teacher needs to maintain the child's motivation. At first, the child will be looking to the adult for encouragement; eventually, problem-solving should become interesting in its own right. • *Marking critical features:* The teacher highlights features of the task that are relevant; this provides information about any inconsistencies between what the child has constructed and what he or she would perceive as a correct construction. • *Demonstration:* Modelling solutions to the task involves completion of a task or explanation of a solution already partly constructed by the child. The aim is that the child will imitate this in an improved form.

Parents routinely act as teachers in the ways outlined above, through rituals and games that are a part of normal adult–child interactions.

Examples of scaffolding:
- When a child is trying to describe a new experience, the adult may guide them in the appropriate use of language.
- During a book-reading session with the child, the adult will demonstrate the process by:
  - engaging the child's attention, e.g. by saying 'Look'
  - simplifying the task by focusing on one question, e.g. 'What's that?'
  - maintaining motivation by encouraging any responses
  - giving information about objects in the book, e.g. 'It's an X'
  - giving appropriate feedback, e.g. 'That's right, it's an X', and encouraging repetition on the part of the child.

Vygotsky's theory of child development

Vygotsky was born in Russia in the same year as Piaget. His study of cognitive development was greatly influenced by the rise of Marxism in the 1920s. Whereas Piaget was an only child and apparently solitary by nature, Vygotsky was one of eight children, growing up in a culture that valued the importance of the social group. He believed that 'what a child can do in co-operation today he can do alone tomorrow'. The main features of Vygotsky's theory are:

Stage	Characteristics
The interrelationship between thought and language	Concepts, language and memory are mental functions that come from the culture and begin with the interaction between the child and another person. Vygotsky maintained that thought is *internalised language*. When small children are playing, they often keep up a running commentary on what is happening: 'And now the train's going round the tower, and it's banging into the tower, and – oh no – the tower's toppling down ...'. Vygotsky calls this an *external monologue*. As time goes on, the external monologue is internalised as thought.
The zone of proximal development (ZPD)	The ZPD (*proximal* meaning 'next') is defined as the difference between problem-solving that the child is capable of performing independently, and problem-solving that he or she is capable of performing with guidance or collaboration. This defines the area in which maturation and development is currently taking place and suggests the appropriate target for instruction. Each child has a zone of proximal development, which is achievable only with the help and encouragement of another person; this could be guidance from an adult or collaboration with more competent peers. This 'expert intervention' can only enable learning if it is far enough ahead of the child's present level to be a challenge but not so far ahead that it is beyond comprehension.
The importance of play	He believed that play provided foundations for children's developing skills that are essential to social, personal and professional activities. Children benefit from play as it allows them to do things beyond what they can do in 'real' life – such as pretend to drive a car. Play is another way through which children can reach their zone of proximal development.
Reconstruction	Children experience the same situations over and over again as they grow, but each time they can deal with them at a higher level and reconstruct them.
The importance of social interactions	Knowledge is not individually constructed but is co-constructed between two people. Remembering, problem solving, planning, and abstract thinking have a social origin. What starts as a social function becomes *internalised*, so that it occurs within the child.
The cultural context	Children use tools that develop from their own culture, such as speech and writing, to help them to function effectively in society. The history of both the culture and the child's experiences are important for understanding cognitive development.

Freud's theory of personality

Freud believed that the structure of personality involves three parts: the *id*, the *ego* and the *superego*.

- The *id* contains the drives that people have. The id wants its wishes immediately and directly fulfilled, and works on the *pleasure principle*, which suggests that all processes operate to achieve the maximum amount of pleasure – and to avoid pain. The id is almost completely unconscious. In the newborn infant, all mental processes are id processes.

- The *ego* is the mediator between the *id* and the *superego*. As the child grows older, reality intervenes and the ego develops. The ego tries to reconcile the wishes of the id, and the moral attitudes of the superego. The ego is governed by the *reality principle*, which suggests that the person gets as much satisfaction from the world as possible. The ego is rational and logical and allows the child to learn that negotiating, asking and explaining more effective ways of satisfying demands than through the id's 'I want'.

- The *superego* contains all of the moral lessons the person has learned in their life; it incorporates ideas of duty, obligation and conscience. At around 4 to 6 years old, the child comes into contact with authority, and the supergo emerges.

Freud's psychosexual stages – a summary

Freud believed that we develop through stages based upon a particular *erogenous zone* – or pleasure zone. During each stage, an unsuccessful completion means that a child becomes fixated on that particular erogenous zone and either over- or under-indulges once he or she becomes an adult.

Stage	Pleasure zone	Description
Oral stage (Birth to 1 year)	**Mouth**	Babies gain satisfaction from putting things into their mouth and sucking. The earliest attachment is usually to the mother as providing oral gratification through feeding. Babies who have not received the optimum amount of oral stimulation – perhaps being weaned too early or too late – become fixated. **Adult behaviour if fixated at this stage**: smoking, nail-biting, over-eating and passivity.
Anal stage (1 to 3 years)	**Anus**	Children have their first encounter with rules and regulations, as they have to learn to be toilet trained; a child has control over retention and expulsion of faeces. Strict potty training is thought to lead to fixation at this stage. **Adult behaviour if fixated at this stage**: obsession with cleanliness, perfection and control (anal retentive). On the opposite end of the spectrum, they may become messy and disorganised (anal expulsive).
Phallic stage (3 to 6 years)	**Genitals**	Boys develop **unconscious** sexual desires for their mother. Because of this, a boy becomes a rival to his father and sees him as competition for the mother's affection. Boys also develop a fear that their father will punish them for these feelings, such as by *castrating* them. This group of feelings is known as Oedipus complex (after the Greek mythology figure who accidentally killed his father and married his mother). The equivalent complex in girls is known as the Electra complex. **Adult behaviour if fixated at this stage**: vanity and recklessness, and their opposites, modesty and cautiousness.
Latency stage (6 to 12 years)	**No specific focus**	Sexual urges remain repressed and children interact and play mostly with same sex peers. Children often develop 'crushes' on same-sex adults. **Fixation does not usually occur at this stage**.
Genital stage (12 to 18 years and adulthood)	**Genitals**	At around puberty, children begin to develop an interest in relationships with the opposite sex, and during this stage reach mature sexual intimacy. **This stage does not cause any fixation**. According to Freud, if people experience difficulties at this stage – and many people do – the damage was done in earlier oral, anal and phallic stages. For example, attraction to the opposite sex can be a source of anxiety at this stage if the person has not successfully resolved the Oedipal or Electra conflict at the phallic stage.

Erikson's theory of psychosocial development

Erikson's theory has eight distinct stages, each with two possible outcomes. Successful completion of each stage results in a healthy personality and successful interactions with others. Failure to complete a stage successfully can result in a reduced ability to complete further stages and therefore a more unhealthy personality and sense of self. These stages, however, can be resolved successfully at a later time.

Stage	Psychosocial relationship
1 Trust vs mistrust **(Birth to 1 year)**	Children begin to learn the ability to trust others based upon the consistency of their caregivers. If trust develops successfully, the child gains confidence and security in the world around him or her and is able to feel secure even when threatened. Unsuccessful completion of this stage can result in an inability to trust, and therefore a sense of fear about the inconsistent world. It may result in anxiety, heightened insecurities and an excessive feeling of mistrust in the world around them.
2 Autonomy vs shame and doubt **(1 to 3 years)**	Children begin to assert their independence, by walking away from their mother, choosing which toy to play with and making choices about what they like to wear, to eat etc. If children in this stage are encouraged and supported in their increased independence, they become more confident and secure in their own ability to survive in the world. If children are criticised, overly controlled or not given the opportunity to assert themselves, they begin to feel inadequate in their ability to survive, and may then lack self-esteem, and feel a sense of shame or doubt in their own abilities.
3 Initiative vs guilt **(3 to 6 years)**	Children assert themselves more frequently. They begin to plan activities, make up games and initiate activities with others. If given this opportunity, children develop a sense of initiative, and feel secure in their ability to lead others and make decisions. However, if this tendency is stifled, either through criticism or control, children develop a sense of guilt. They may feel like a nuisance to others and will therefore remain followers, lacking in self-initiative.
4 Industry vs inferiority **(6 to puberty)**	Children begin to develop a sense of pride in their accomplishments. They initiate projects, see them through to completion and feel good about what they have achieved. During this time, teachers play an increased role in the child's development. If children are encouraged and reinforced for their initiative, they begin to feel industrious and feel confident in their ability to achieve goals. If this initiative is not encouraged, the child begins to feel inferior, doubting his or her own abilities, and therefore may not reach his or her potential.
5 Identity vs role confusion **(Adolescence: 12 to 18 years)**	Children/young people are becoming more independent, and begin to look at the future in terms of career, relationships, families etc. During this period, they explore possibilities and begin to form their own identity based upon the outcome of their explorations. This sense of who they are can be stalled, which results in a sense of confusion ('I don't know what I want to be when I grow up') about themselves and their role in the world.
6 Intimacy vs isolation **(Young adulthood: 20s)**	People explore relationships leading towards longer-term commitments with someone other than a family member. Successful completion can lead to comfortable relationships and a sense of commitment, security, and care within a relationship. Avoiding intimacy and fearing commitment and relationships can lead to isolation, loneliness and sometimes depression.
7 Generativity vs stagnation **(Mature adulthood: late 20s to 50s)**	People establish careers, settle down within a relationship, begin their own families and develop a sense of community. By failing to achieve these objectives, they become stagnant and feel unproductive.
8 Ego integrity vs despair **(Old age: 50s and beyond)**	People contemplate their accomplishments and are able to develop integrity if they see themselves as leading a successful life. If they see their lives as unproductive, feel guilt about the past or feel that they did not accomplish their life goals, they become dissatisfied with life and develop despair, often leading to depression and hopelessness.

Bowlby's theory of maternal deprivation and attachment

Bowlby stated that a child's personality development is achieved through a **close continuous relationship** with his or her mother. These are the main principles of Bowlby's theory:

- The first five years of life are the most important in a person's development.

- A child's relationship with its parents (in particular with the mother) has an enormous effect on the child's overall development.

- Separation from a parent, particularly from the mother, is a major cause of psychological trauma in childhood.

- Such separation and consequent psychological trauma has long-lasting effects on the overall development of the child.

- The attachment is *monotropic*. This means that it is established between the infant and one other person.

- There is a critical period for attachment formation. Bowlby thought that the period between 6 months and 3 years was critical for attachment formation. The child *must* form an attachment by about 6 months after which, until around 3 years, she or he has a strong need to be continuously with or close to her or his main carer (usually the mother). Any obstacle to the forming of an attachment, or any subsequent disruption of the relationship, constitutes *maternal deprivation*.

- The *secure attachment* and continuous relationship a child needs is far more likely to be provided within her or his natural family than anywhere else.

There has been confusion over the terms **bonding** and **attachment**. Bonding has at times been portrayed as an almost mystical experience for mothers following the birth of their child. While some mothers do have this experience, many do not. Attachment is a two-way process which develops over time. Bowlby did not say that the most important attachment figure must be the natural mother; he did stress, however, that babies need one central person who is the mother figure. Both the primary caregiver and the infant are active participants in this process. The key factor for the caregiver is sensitive responsiveness – the ability to attune to the child and respond to their signals. The child's responsiveness is also an important contributor to the process. Attachment problems are more likely to arise with 'difficult' babies.

adolescence The period of psychological and social transition between childhood and adulthood, basically covering the teenage years.

animism The belief that all objects possess consciousness.

anterior fontanelle A diamond-shaped soft area at the front of the head, just above the brow. It is a temporary gap between the bones of the head, and is covered by a tough membrane – often you can see the baby's pulse beating beneath the skin. The fontanelle closes between 12 and 18 months of age, when the bones fuse together.

articulation A person's actual pronunciation of words.

attachment An enduring emotional bond that an infant forms with a specific person. Often the first attachment is to the mother, some time between the ages of 6 and 9 months.

attention deficit disorder (ADD) A behavioural disorder characterised by an inability to concentrate on tasks. In attention deficit hyperactivity disorder (ADHD), inability to concentrate is accompanied or replaced by hyperactive and impulsive behaviour.

autism (autistic spectrum disorder) A rare developmental disorder which impairs a child's understanding of, and her or his ability to relate to, the environment.

bonding A term used to denote the feelings of love and responsibility that parents have for their babies.

British Sign Language (BSL) One of the languages used by those with a hearing impairment. To conduct a conversation, language users make **gestures** involving movements of their hands, arms, eyes, face and body.

casting Repeatedly throwing objects to the floor, in play or rejection.

cataract The loss of transparency of the crystalline lens of the eye.

central nervous system (CNS) The brain and the spinal cord, which are the main control centres of the body.

cerebral palsy A general term for disorders of movement and posture resulting from damage to the child's developing brain.

cleft palate A hole or split in the palate (the roof of the mouth).

coeliac disease A condition in which the lining of the small intestine is damaged by gluten, a protein found in wheat and certain other cereals.

cognitive (intellectual) Related to the ideas and thinking of the child. Cognition emphasises that children are aware, active learners, and that understanding is an important part of intellectual life.

comfort object (transitional object) An object, such as a blanket, a piece of cloth or a teddy, to which a child becomes especially attached.

communication Facial expression, body language, gestures, and verbal or sign language; talking about feelings, ideas and relationships using signs or words. (Language involves both **reception** – understanding – and **expression**.)

concept An overall idea formed in the mind, which is based on and links past, present and future ideas that share some attributes. Thus a child may sit on a variety of actual chairs, but the concept of 'a chair' is an idea that develops in the child's mind.

conservation The concept that objects remain the same in basic ways, such as their weight or number, even when there are external changes in their shape or arrangement.

co-operative play Play in which children take account of other children's actions or roles within their play together – for instance, one might be the baby, the other the nurse, and the nurse might give medical treatment to the baby.

cradle test *See* **Otoacoustic Emissions Testing**.

creative play *See* **imaginative play**.

creativity The ability to make something from an idea one has imagined, for example a dance, a model, a poem or a mathematical equation; the process of creating something.

Down's syndrome A genetic anomaly, which results in children having learning difficulties and characteristic physical features.

dynamic tripod grasp Using the thumb and two fingers in a grip closely resembling the adult grip of a pencil or pen. *Compare* **primitive tripod grasp**.

dyslexia A specific reading disability, characterised by difficulty in coping with written symbols.

dyspraxia An immaturity of the brain such that some messages are not transmitted to the body. Children with dyspraxia often show behavioural difficulties and may be hyperactive.

echolalia The tendency of a child to echo the last words spoken by an adult.

egocentric Self-centred, or viewing things from one's own standpoint.

ejaculation The process of ejecting semen from the penis; it is usually accompanied by orgasm as a result of sexual stimulation. It may also occur spontaneously during sleep (called a nocturnal emission or 'wet dream').

empathy Awareness of another person's emotional state, and the ability to share the experience with that person.

epididymis A storage chamber in the male's body, which is attached to each testicle. This is where sperm cells are nourished and mature.

erection The penis becomes stiff and hard due to increased blood flow. Erections may happen in response to physical or emotional stimulation, or sometimes an erection happens for no reason at all.

evaluate To find out or judge the value of something.

expression Communication of what one thinks, feels or means, by word, facial expression, gesture or sign language.

expressive speech The words a person produces.

extension Stretching out.

fallopian tubes Narrow tubes that are connected to the uterus. The fringes of the fallopian tube catch the egg cell when it is released from the ovary, and the egg cell then slowly travels from the ovary to the uterus.

fantasy play Play in which children role-play situations they do not fully know about but which might happen to them one day, such as going to hospital or travelling to the moon in a space rocket.

fine manipulative skills Skills involving precise use of the hands and fingers in pointing, drawing, using a knife and fork, using chopsticks, writing, doing up shoelaces and the like.

fine motor skills Skills including **gross manipulative skills**, which involve single limb movements, and **fine manipulative skills**, which involve precise movements of the hands and fingers.

flexion Bending.

gay A term used to describe men and women who are sexually attracted to people of their own sex.

gender identity The psychological sense a person has of being male or female.

genitals The external sex organs.

gesture Any movement intended to convey meaning.

giftedness Having unusually great ability over a wide range of skills.

gross manipulative skills Skills involving single limb movements, usually of the arm, for example in throwing, catching and sweeping arm movements.

gross motor skills Skills involving the use of the large muscles in the body; they include walking, running, climbing and the like.

growth (centile) chart A graph or chart used to plot the growth measurements (height and weight) of babies and children.

growth spurt A rapid growth of bone and muscle occurring at various ages from infancy to puberty.

heterosexism The belief and practice that heterosexuality is the only natural form of sexuality, and the belief that being heterosexual is better than being homosexual.

heterosexual Feeling sexually attracted to people of the opposite sex.

holistic Tending to see something in the round, for example seeing a child as a whole person, emotionally, intellectually, socially, physically, morally, culturally and spiritually.

holophrase The expression of a whole idea in a single word: thus 'car' may mean 'Give me the car' or 'Look at the car'.

homophobia Negative or fearful attitudes to homosexuality.

homosexual Feeling sexually attracted to people of the same sex.

hormones Chemical messengers created by glands that control specific things that happen in the body.

hypothalamus An area of the brain responsible for controlling functions such as regulating fluid balance, body temperature, sleep, food intake and the development of the body during puberty.

ICT Information communication technology: the computing and communications facilities and features that variously support teaching, learning and a range of activities in education. The most obvious example of this is computers, but it can also mean televisions, videos, DVDs, CDs, cassette recorders, telephones, musical keyboards and fax machines.

imagination The ability to form new ideas, which, though they may emerge from first-hand experiences of life, go beyond what one has experienced.

imaginative play (creative play) Play in which children draw on their own real-life experiences and rearrange them – for instance, they might make a pretend swimming pool from wooden blocks and then play out a rescue scene in which a child is saved from drowning in the pool by a lifeguard.

inclusive care and education The integration of disabled children into mainstream settings such as nursery schools, day nurseries, schools and family centres.

intellectual *See* **cognitive**.

labile Having rapidly fluctuating moods, such as cheerful one moment and angry the next.

lesbian Refers to women who are sexually attracted to other women. The word 'gay' can also be used.

LGBT An abbreviation for lesbian, gay, bisexual and transgender people.

literacy The ability to read and write: writing involves putting spoken language into a written code; reading involves decoding the written code into language.

Makaton A method of sign language that uses a combination of manual signs, graphic symbols and speech (the Makaton Vocabulary) to support spoken English.

menarche The first menstrual period.

meningitis Inflammation of the meninges membranes that enclose the brain and spinal cord.

menstruation The process by which the lining of the uterus is shed periodically as menstrual flow. It usually happens about once a month except during pregnancy.

metacognition A loosely used term describing an individual's knowledge of their own thinking processes. It means that you know both what you know and how you manage to remember and learn.

motor development Growth and change in the ability to carry out physical activities, such as walking, running or riding a bicycle.

nocturnal emission An ejaculation of semen that happens while a boy is sleeping. It is sometimes called a 'wet dream', and is nature's way of making room for new sperm cells that are made.

norm An average or typical state or ability, used with others as a framework for assessing development. Norms are the result of observations by many professionals in the field of child development.

normative Relating to norms or averages.

object permanence The recognition that an object continues to exist even when temporarily out of sight.

observation The process of watching accurately and taking notice.

oestrogen The main female sex hormone produced by the ovaries.

orgasm A pleasurable physical or emotional response to sexual stimulation; it is also known as a sexual climax.

Otoacoustic Emissions Testing (OAE, or cradle test) A hearing test. It is often called the 'cradle test' because it is performed on newborn babies.

ovaries Two small organs inside a female's body where egg cells are produced and stored. Each ovary is about the size of a walnut, and there is one on each side of the uterus. The ovaries also produce the hormones oestrogen and progesterone.

ovulation The release of an egg cell by an ovary. This process usually occurs at the midpoint of the menstrual cycle.

ovum Another name for the female egg cell. It is smaller than a grain of salt.

paediatrician A qualified doctor who specialises in treating children.

palmar grasp Using the whole hand to grasp an object.

parallel play Play in which one child plays alongside another child, but without interacting with the other child.

penis The male reproductive organ involved in sexual intercourse and elimination of urine.

perception The process by which events and information in the environment are transformed into an experience of objects, sounds, events and the like.

period The days when menstruation is taking place.

personality The total combination of mental and behavioural characteristics that make each individual recognisably unique. Personality is affected by children's experiences of life and other people, as well as by the child's natural temperament.

Picture Exchange Communication System (PECS) A communication system using picture symbols – rather than words or signing – within a social context.

pincer grip Using the thumb and fingers to grasp an object

pituitary gland A small gland at the base of the brain, which is responsible for controlling the hormones that affect growth, metabolism and maturation.

posterior fontanelle A small triangular-shaped soft area near the crown of the head. It is a temporary gap between the bones of the head, and is much smaller and less noticeable than the **anterior fontanelle**. It usually closes by 6 to 8 weeks of age.

pretend play Play in which an action or object is given a symbolic meaning other than that from real life, such as when a clothes peg is used to represent a door key, or a large box to represent a boat.

primary sexual characteristics The penis and sperm in males and the vagina and ovaries in females. *Compare* **secondary sexual characteristics**.

primitive reflexes Automatic reactions to particular changes in surroundings – present in the newborn baby, and thought to be vital for the infant's survival. Reflexes give an indication of the baby's general condition and the normal functioning of the **central nervous system**. *See also* **reflex**.

primitive tripod grasp Grasping objects by use of the thumb and two fingers. Compare **dynamic tripod grasp**.

progesterone A female hormone.

prone Lying on one's face, or front downward. Compare **supine**.

proprioception The sense that tells infants where the mobile parts of their body (such as their legs) are in relation to the rest of them.

prostate gland A male gland at the base of the bladder. It contributes a thin, milky fluid that makes up the largest part of the semen.

puberty The stage of growth in which a child's body turns into the body of an adult. The child or young person experiences physical, hormonal, and sexual changes and becomes capable of reproduction. It is associated with rapid growth and the appearance of secondary sexual characteristics.

reception (of language) Listening to or watching and understanding language.

receptive speech The words a person understands.

reflex An automatic response to a stimulus. *See also* **primitive reflexes**.

role-play Play in which 'pretend' symbols are used together with an activity – for example, a child pretends that a box is a car and then 'drives' to the shops.

scaffolding A term used by, among others, Bruner, for describing the support given to a child in order for him or her to construct and extend skills to higher levels of competence, during which the scaffolding is slowly removed.

schema Children's patterns of learning; linked actions and behaviours that the child can generalise and use in a variety of different situations, e.g. up, down, in, out etc.

scrotum The outside sac of loose skin under the penis that holds the testicles.

secondary sexual characteristics Traits that distinguish the two sexes of a species, but which are not directly part of the reproductive system, e.g. enlarged breasts in females and pubic hair in both sexes.

self-concept How a child sees himself or herself; how the child believes others see him or her.

self-esteem The way a child feels about herself or himself: good feelings lead to high self-esteem, bad feelings lead to low self-esteem.

semen A milky white fluid made by the seminal vesicles and prostate gland. This fluid mixes with the sperm cells during an ejaculation. A teaspoonful or more of semen comes out of the penis during an ejaculation.

seminal vesicle One of two glands located behind the male bladder, which secrete a fluid that forms part of semen.

sensation Being aware of having an experience, through seeing, smelling, hearing, touching, tasting or moving (kinaesthesia).

sexual intercourse The erect penis of the male entering the vagina of the female.

sexual orientation An enduring emotional, romantic and sexual attraction to a particular sex.

Signalong A method of signing (using gestures and symbols) used with children who have communication difficulties.

small-world play Play that involves the use of miniature objects, such as doll's houses, toy farms and zoos, dinosaurs and play-people.

smooth pursuit *See* **tracking**.

socialisation The process by which children learn the culture or way of life of the society into which they have been born.

solitary play (solo play) Play in which a child plays alone, exploring and experimenting with objects.

spectator play Play in which children watch what others do, but do not join in.

sperm The microscopic cells produced by a male that contains the genes from the father. A sperm cell from the father must join with an egg cell from the mother for a baby to be created.

spina bifida A condition in which one or more of the vertebrae in the backbone fail to form, as a result of which the spinal cord may be damaged. Spina bifida may be mild; in its severest form, however, it can cause widespread paralysis and a wide range of physical disabilities.

supine Lying on one's back, or face upwards. *Compare* **prone**.

symbolism Making one thing stand for another.

talipes A condition in which the foot is not in the correct alignment with the leg; it is sometimes called 'club foot'.

telegraphic speech (telegraphese) The abbreviation of a sentence such that only the crucial words are spoken, as in a telegram – for instance, 'Where daddy going?' or 'Shut door'.

temperament The style of behaviour that comes naturally, as, for example, a general tendency to be relaxed or excitable.

testes The medical name for **testicles**. (The singular is testis.)

testicles The main male reproductive glands in which sperm are produced. The testicles also produce the main male hormone, testosterone.

testosterone A male sex hormone, which causes a boy's body to develop into a man's. Testosterone is responsible for promoting more muscle mass, a deeper voice and facial hair.

tracking (smooth pursuit) The smooth movements made by the eyes in following the track of a moving object.

transitional object *See* **comfort object**.

transsexual Having a body with one set of sexual characteristics but feeling emotionally that you are the opposite sex.

uterus Another name for the womb.

ventral suspension Supported in a prone position with a hand under the abdomen.

weaning The introduction of solid food to a baby's diet, at the age of 4–6 months.

References and further reading

Bee, H. (1992). *The Developing Child*
(New York: HarperCollins).

Bruce, T. (1996). *Helping Young Children to Play*
(London: Hodder & Stoughton).

Bruce, T. and Meggitt, C. (2002). *Child Care and Education*
(London: Hodder & Stoughton).

Cole, M. & Cole, S.R. (1993). *The Development of Children*
(New York: Scientific American).

Einon, D. (1985). *Creative Play*
(London: Penguin Books).

Gopnik, A., Meltzoff, A. and Kuhl, P. (2000). *How Babies Think: The Science of Childhood*
(London: Weidenfeld & Nicholson).

Karmiloff-Smith, A. (1994). *Baby It's You*
(London: Ebury Press).

Landsdowne, R. and Walker, M. (1996). *Your Child's Development from Birth to Adolescence*
(London: Frances Lincoln).

Meggitt, C. (2001). *Baby and Child Health*
(Oxford: Heinemann Educational).

Nyssen, C. (2003). *Baby Massage*
(Oxford: Heinemann Educational).

Sheridan, M.D. (1997). *From Birth to Five*
(London: Routledge).

Thomson, H. and Meggitt, C. (1997). *Human Growth and Development*
(London: Hodder & Stoughton).

Useful addresses and websites

Action for Sick Children
National Children's Bureau
8, Wakley Street
London
EC1V 7QE

Tel: 020 7843 6444
Website: www.actionforsickchildren.org

Advisory Centre for Education (ACE)
1c Aberdeen Studios
22 Highbury Grove
London
N5 2DQ

Tel: 020 7704 3370
Website: www.ace-ed.org.uk

Association for Spina Bifida and Hydracephalus (ASBAH)
Head Office
42 Park Road
Peterborough
PE1 2UQ

Tel: 01733 555988
Website: www.asbah.org

Child Growth Foundation
2 Mayfield Avenue
Chiswick
London
W4 1PW

Tel: 020 8995 0257
Website: www.childgrowthfoundation.org

Contact a Family
(Contact a Family helps families who care for children with any disability or special need.)
209–211 City Road
London
EC1V 1JN

Tel: 020 7608 8700
Website: www.cafamily.org.uk

Council for Disabled Children
Wakeley Street
London
EC1V 7QE

Tel: 020 7843 6061
Website: www.ncb.org.uk

Cystic Fibrosis Trust
11 London Road
Bromley
BR1 1BY

Tel: 020 8464 7211
Website: www.cftrust.org.uk

Down's Syndrome Association
Langdon Down Centre
2a Langdon Park
Teddington
TW11 9PS

Tel: 0845 230 0372
Website: www.downs-syndrome.org.uk

Dyslexia Institute
Park House, Wick Road
Egham
Surrey
W20 0HH

Tel: 01784 222300
Website: www.dyslexia-inst.org.uk

Home-Start UK
(Home-Start schemes offer friendship, support and practical advice to families in difficulties with children under 5 in their homes.)
2 Salisbury Road
Leicester
LE1 7QR

Tel: 0116 233 9955
Website: www.homestart.org.uk

I CAN
(I CAN helps children with a communication disability.)
4 Dyer's Building
Holborn
London
EC1N 2QP

Tel: 0845 225 4071
Website: www.ican.org.uk

KIDS
(KIDS helps disabled children to get the most out of life.)
6 Aztec Row
Berners Road
London
N1 0PW

Tel: 020 7359 3635
Website: www.kids.org.uk

MENCAP
(Royal Society for Mentally Handicapped Children and Adults.)
MENCAP National Centre
123 Golden Lane
London
EC1Y 0RT

Tel: 020 7454 0454
Website: www.mencap.org.uk

Muscular Dystrophy Group of Great Britain and Northern Ireland
Head Office
7–11 Prescott Place
London
SW4 6BS

Tel: 020 7720 8055
Website: www.muscular-dystrophy.org

National Asthma Campaign
Asthma UK
Summit House
70 Wilson Street
London
EC2A 2DB

Tel: 020 7786 4990
Website: www.asthma.org.uk

National Autistic Society
393 City Road
London
EC1V 1NG

Tel: 020 7833 2299
Website: www.nas.org.uk

National Deaf Children's Society (NDCS)
15 Dufferin Street
London
EC1Y 8UR

Tel: 020 7490 8656
Website: www.ndcs.org.uk

National Eczema Society (NES)
Hill House
Highgate Hill
London
N19 5NA

Tel: 020 7281 3553
Website: www.eczema.org

Pre-School Learning Alliance
Kings Cross Road
London
WC1X 9LL

Tel: 020 7833 0991
Website: www.pre-school.org.uk

REACH
(The Association for Children with Hand or Arm Deficiency.)
PO Box 54
Helston
Cornwall
TR13 8WD

Tel: 0845 1306 22512
Website: www.reach.org.uk

Royal Institute for the Blind (RNIB)
224 Great Portland Street
London
W1N 6AA

Tel: 020 7388 1266
Website: www.rnib.org.uk

SCOPE
(The association for people with cerebral palsy.)
6 Market Road,
London
N7 9PW

Tel: 020 7619 7100
Website: www.scope.org.uk

SEBDA
(SEBDA serves the interests of children and young people experiencing difficulties in their social, emotional and behavioural development.)
Church House
1 St Andrew's View
Penrith
Cumbria
CA11 7YF

Tel: 01768 210 510
Website: www.sebda.org

SENSE
(National Deaf-Blind and Rubella Association.)
11–13 Clifton Terrace
Finsbury Park
London
N4 3SR

Tel: 020 7272 7774
Website: www.sense.org.uk

Use the pages provided to make your own notes.